EDUCATION POLICY ANALYSIS 2004

ORGANISATION FOR ECONOMIC CO-OPERATION AND DEVELOPMENT

ORGANISATION FOR ECONOMIC CO-OPERATION AND DEVELOPMENT

The OECD is a unique forum where the governments of 30 democracies work together to address the economic, social and environmental challenges of globalisation. The OECD is also at the forefront of efforts to understand and to help governments respond to new developments and concerns, such as corporate governance, the information economy and the challenges of an ageing population. The Organisation provides a setting where governments can compare policy experiences, seek answers to common problems, identify good practice and work to co-ordinate domestic and international policies.

The OECD member countries are: Australia, Austria, Belgium, Canada, the Czech Republic, Denmark, Finland, France, Germany, Greece, Hungary, Iceland, Ireland, Italy, Japan, Korea, Luxembourg, Mexico, the Netherlands, New Zealand, Norway, Poland, Portugal, the Slovak Republic, Spain, Sweden, Switzerland, Turkey, the United Kingdom and the United States. The Commission of the European Communities takes part in the work of the OECD.

OECD Publishing disseminates widely the results of the Organisation's statistics gathering and research on economic, social and environmental issues, as well as the conventions, guidelines and standards agreed by its members.

This work is published on the responsibility of the Secretary-General of the OECD. The opinions expressed and arguments employed herein do not necessarily reflect the official views of the Organisation or of the governments of its member countries.

Publié en français sous le titre :
Analyse des politiques d'éducation
ÉDITION 2004

FOREWORD

This edition of *Education Policy Analysis* addresses a number of significant current policy issues that spring from the OECD's key strategic objectives in the area of education. It links work on education to work conducted elsewhere within the OECD (more particularly within the Directorate for Science, Technology and Industry and the OECD Centre for Tax Policy and Administration). In doing this, *Education Policy Analysis* reflects the emphasis upon closer policy connections that was a strong theme of the inaugural meeting of the chief executives of OECD education systems that was held in Dublin in February 2003.

Education Policy Analysis forms part of the programme of work of the OECD's Education Committee and of the Directorate for Education. It is a collaborative effort between member governments, the national experts that work with the OECD, and the OECD Secretariat. The series is prepared by the Education and Training Policy Division under the direction of Abrar Hasan.

The principal contributions to this issue were made by Richard Sweet and Donald Hirsch as editors, Norton Grubb (Chapter 1), Richard Sweet (Chapter 2), David Istance (Chapter 3) and Gregory Wurzburg (Chapter 4). Statistical support for Chapter 2 was provided by Christian Monseur and John Cresswell. Co-ordination and copy editing were the responsibility of Delphine Grandrieux. Fung-Kwan Tam was responsible for the layout design. Dianne Fowler and Patricia Prinsen-Geerligs were responsible for administration. Valuable comments on draft chapters were provided by members of the OECD Secretariat, members of the OECD Education Committee, members of the Governing Board of the Centre for Educational Research and Innovation, and national co-ordinators of the Indicators of National Education Systems project. The views expressed in this publication do not, however, represent those of OECD member governments.

The publication is issued on the responsibility of the Secretary-General of the OECD.

Barry Mc Gaw
Director for Education

TABLE OF CONTENTS

List of boxes, figures and tables

BOXES

FIGURES

EXECUTIVE SUMMARY

Revisiting a theme that was first examined by the OECD some 30 years ago, Chapter 1 takes a fresh look at the place of alternatives to the traditional university within national tertiary education systems. Chapter 2 reviews a range of OECD work on the educational uses of ICT, draws some cautionary lessons, and suggests a number of conditions needed to get better returns from national investments in educational ICT. Chapter 3 discusses a topic that has hitherto not been systematically treated in the OECD's educational work: the important role that schools should play in laying the foundations for national lifelong learning frameworks. Finally, Chapter 4 breaks new ground by looking at some of the policy issues that need to be considered in using tax policy as an instrument to advance lifelong learning. The volume contains an Annex that summarises recent educational policy developments in OECD countries.

ALTERNATIVES TO UNIVERSITIES REVISITED

Universities no longer have a monopoly over the provision of tertiary education. In a number of countries, over one-third of enrolments at this level are now in other types of institution, and in a few it is the majority. Non-university institutions providing tertiary education vary hugely in character, ranging from vocational colleges providing a mix of upper secondary and short-cycle tertiary courses, to polytechnic institutions teaching four-year courses at degree level. Yet two common imperatives have influenced the growth of such institutions in OECD countries. The first is to create extra capacity to expand the overall supply of tertiary education. The second is to diversify what is on offer, in terms for example of the range of courses, their accessibility and the closeness of links with employers and the wider community.

The non-university institutions that provide tertiary education **vary substantially in their purposes.** Some, like the German *Fachhochschulen*, are narrowly focused on providing vocationally-oriented degrees. Others, such as community colleges in North America, teach for a wider range of levels and purposes. Three key dimensions of these purposes are:

- *The extent of vocational orientation.* In many countries, non-university institutions have developed from vocational or technical institutes, and they commonly offer fewer courses of general programmes, for example in the humanities, than universities. Yet some types of institution also have a mission to help improve access to universities, and in these cases, the vocational orientation is less pervasive. Such institutions include not just multi-purpose ones in North America and Australia, but also French *Instituts universitaires de technologie* (IUTs), which offer a standardised two-year qualification.

- *The levels of education provided.* In English-speaking countries, a number of institutions offer a range of courses from upper secondary through to degree-level courses. In a number of German-speaking and Nordic countries, on the other hand, non-university tertiary institutions normally teach only advanced courses, to the equivalent of a first university degree, with lower levels of education for adults being provided elsewhere.

- *Community orientation.* Many countries now have networks of non-university institutions that are more numerous than universities, and therefore more geographically dispersed. This both improves local access and in some cases serves communities in other ways; for example by conducting research that is oriented to local or regional economic development.

Non-university tertiary providers fit into an overall system of provision in a variety of ways. Sometimes tiers of institutions with different status are clearly distinguished, as in binary or tripartite systems, but the picture can be more complex where the types of courses and qualifications in different categories of institution overlap. In some countries, notably Germany and Finland, non-university institutions have a key role in driving the overall expansion of tertiary provision. However, in expanding access they do not always stand alone, and in many countries the way in which they articulate with universities – including the conditions for transfer across institutions – is critical.

Another key element in their role in an expanding system is **their relatively lower funding per student in most countries**. In some countries this is little over half of the amount spent in universities. This can partly but not wholly be explained by programme differences, and raises questions about equity of provision. In some but not all countries this is partly compensated by the fact that students in non-university institutions are charged lower fees. There is a need to think more carefully about how to develop an equitable cost and charging structure in a complex, heterogeneous system of tertiary education. This also raises issues of quality, including the quality of teaching, which in principle ought to be the focus of non-research oriented institutions but in practice has received insufficient attention. Do non-university tertiary institutions offer value for money? This is hard to calculate with available data, but the evidence shows that returns are at best uneven, varying greatly across institutions and courses.

These alternatives to universities will certainly play a large role in tertiary provision in the future. Yet **their precise role within the system is still being resolved**, with a range of strategies open to them, whether becoming more like universities or emphasising their differences. Education authorities too will need to think carefully about what roles they wish these institutions to play in the tertiary education system.

GETTING RETURNS FROM INVESTING IN EDUCATIONAL ICT

Since the mid-1990s, **information and communication technologies (ICT) have been seen by many as an integral part of a strategy to improve teaching and learning**. This is more ambitious than earlier uses of computers, for example as supplementary teaching aids or to reduce teaching costs. But are policies to use ICT to transform education working? What investments have been made, what kinds of return have they brought and what barriers remain to the effective deployment of ICT?

All OECD countries have invested heavily in ICT in schools, although the presence of equipment still varies greatly across countries. In 2003, the number of 15-year-old students per computer in different countries ranged from 3 to 25. These differences cannot be explained simply by variations in wealth or overall education spending. However, most schools now have access to the Internet, and as the physical availability of technology becomes more pervasive, attention is increasingly turning to how ICT can be integrated into teaching and learning, in order to produce better learning outcomes.

In assessing the return on ICT investment, one needs to bear in mind that ICT can be used to improve information management within schools and to upgrade students' ICT skills as well as to transform teaching and learning. Depending on which of these goals is considered important, the style of investment in ICT will differ, so it is hard to measure the overall return.

One indication is the extent to which students use computers. In some countries at least one in three 15-year-olds uses computers in schools less than once a month, although in a few, usage has become routine: two out of three students in Denmark, Hungary and the United Kingdom use computers several times a week or daily. **The level of investment in equipment is not a good**

predictor of how much it will be used, although unsurprisingly the countries with particularly large numbers of students per computer have below-average usage. Most commonly, students use computers for email and browsing the Internet – both of which may have educational benefits. The number of students using specific educational software appears to be declining.

Does ICT improve learning outcomes? The evidence on this is imprecise, although **some research indicates that greater use of technology can raise performance**. It is encouraging that the schools with the greatest concentrations of low achievers are at least as well endowed with computers as the average school, and in some countries more so. This is in contrast to the distribution of computers in homes, which greatly favours more advantaged students: thus **schools can help counter the effects of the digital divide**. However, in schools where computers are scarce, low achievers have a lower than average tendency to access them.

Low achieving students are just as interested in using computers as other students, but on average less confident. Nevertheless, case study evidence indicates that **ICT can be used effectively to raise students' interest and confidence in learning**.

The barriers that prevent ICT producing desired results in schools can include lack of sufficient physical resources, regular technical support and maintenance. However, most fundamentally, the barriers include the ways in which classroom learning, schools and education systems are organised. **Principals highlight in particular four obstacles to reaching their ICT development goals**, each of which affects at least 60% of upper secondary school students across the OECD:

• Difficulty in integrating computers into classroom instruction.

• Problems in scheduling enough computer time.

• Teachers' lack of knowledge in using computers as a teaching tool.

• Teachers not having enough time to prepare lessons that use computers.

To overcome such barriers, teachers need to be well trained and prepared to use computers effectively, but this will not be enough if the organisation of schools and pedagogies remain unchanged. Case study evidence shows that, whether ICT is a trigger for change or a tool that enables it to take place, **there needs to be a close interaction between the use of computers and other aspects of school development**. Thus, just as is the case in business, the potential of ICT will only be realised if its introduction is combined effectively with other kinds of innovation.

HOW WELL DO SCHOOLS CONTRIBUTE TO LIFELONG LEARNING?

Lifelong learning is a concept that was originally applied to the continuation of learning beyond initial education. It **now signifies an approach to learning throughout life, including at school**. The OECD has defined a framework for lifelong learning that contains four elements. Each of these has implications for school education:

• Organised learning should be *systemic and inter-connected*. School education should therefore be linked to learning at other stages of life.

• The learner should be *central to the learning process*. This is a particularly challenging requirement in compulsory education.

- There should be an emphasis on *the motivation to learn* – another challenging demand for initial education, from which many become disaffected.

- Recognition should be given to the *multiple objectives of education*, rather than concentrating only on economic or instrumentalist goals.

How well school systems measure up to the ideals of lifelong learning can be analysed at three levels: the individual student, the school as an organisation and the school system.

At the level of the student, **school systems need to ensure** not only that students complete their schooling, but also **that they nurture the competences that students will need in adult life.** Insofar as completion of secondary school provides a foundation for lifelong learning, progress has been encouraging. In most OECD countries, the vast majority of young people now leave school with an upper secondary qualification. But what kinds of skills and dispositions have they acquired when they do so? The PISA survey has investigated the extent to which they have some of the key knowledge and skills that they will need in adult life. Its findings show that there is much still to be achieved. For example, in many countries at least one-third of students cannot perform reading tasks of moderate complexity, a vital skill needed in pursuing lifelong learning.

Yet **one must also look at a wider range of outcomes of education, not only cognitive abilities**. The OECD's Definition and Selection of Competences (DeSeCo) project has identified three types of competency needed in adult life: using a range of knowledge-related tools including language and technology; interacting effectively with other people; and exercising personal autonomy. While these competences cannot always be accurately measured, PISA has provided some indicators of whether school students are well prepared for lifelong learning in different ways. One measurable aspect of **autonomy** is the extent to which students control their own learning, and those who do are more likely to perform well at school. On the **motivation**al side, the results are encouraging in showing that most 15-year-old students feel as though they "belong" at school, although a significant minority do not. A striking aspect of this evidence is that in some countries where students show high achievement, relatively large numbers feel unhappy at school, and this could have implications for the likelihood that they carry on learning later in life.

The second level at which lifelong learning principles apply is that of **schools**, which **need to become learning organisations, with students at the centre of learning**. This involves not just a willingness of teachers to learn and to change, but school-led innovation that changes learning cultures. This requires education to emulate conditions that have allowed innovation to succeed elsewhere. One of these is the application of research knowledge. A second is practitioner collaboration to find new ways of doing things, requiring better teacher networks and incentives for teachers to work together. A third is the creation of a "modular" innovation system that simultaneously permits local difference and joins local innovation to other parts of the system. A final driver of innovation is the effective use of information and communication technologies. In all of these respects, there are barriers to educational change, yet in each there is potential for progress.

Finally, at the system level, lifelong learning requires a connection between schooling and other aspects of education and training throughout people's lives. **A key issue** here **is whether the continued expansion of initial education is necessarily desirable**. While it provides a good foundation for lifelong learning, it also potentially "front loads" education even more than in the past. There is no single solution to this conundrum, but countries need to think carefully about the timing of when opportunities are available. Beyond initial upper secondary education, there may need to be more of a level playing field in supporting opportunities to study at different ages.

TAXATION AND LIFELONG LEARNING

The arrangements that allow people to continue learning throughout their lives remain poorly developed. In particular, factors which make it economically worthwhile to invest in learning, and which ensure that the financial means to do so are available, are often weak beyond initial schooling. **Potentially, tax policy is one way to strengthen** these **economic and financial incentives**. Yet whereas taxation has been used to influence other forms of investment, it has only rarely been used deliberately to influence lifelong learning. This does not mean that it has no influence. However this influence has in general been accidental rather than planned.

The case for using taxation, as well as other fiscal instruments, **to influence learning investment is that the benefits of learning are shared between society, employers and individuals**: therefore unsupported private coverage of the cost of learning will lead to a sub-optimal level of investment. Yet adult learning, unlike initial education, is at best unevenly supported by the state. How can the cost be more systematically shared? Recent OECD discussions about existing co-financing arrangements have found that tax policy is embedded, deliberately or otherwise, in many such schemes. The challenge identified in a recent OECD conference on the subject is to make such approaches more systemic across government, with the active collaboration of ministries of finance.

Tax systems have multiple objectives. The first of these is to raise money for public spending without unduly distorting the economy; promoting activities of social benefit can also be significant. **There are two main channels through which tax policy may influence investment in lifelong learning**:

- First, *through the taxation of revenues* from the sale of learning services. If learning is regarded as an investment, an objective should be to ensure that these revenues are taxed in the same way as other investments to maintain neutrality. This also requires all providers to be taxed equally. One of the commonest ways in which this principle is breached is by taxing learning services provided by for-profit organisations, but not those provided by public and other non-profit-making bodies.

- Second, *through the tax treatment of expenditure* on investment in learning. There are many ways in which individual and corporate spending on learning can be exempted from tax. However it is hard to produce neutral support across the board. The common pattern is to favour learning for current employment over future employment (however this is being relaxed in some cases), to favour more measurable classroom activities over on-the-job learning; and to favour expenditure by firms over expenditure by individuals. Moreover, tax concessions are worth more for better-off individuals and firms – those whose marginal tax rates are relatively high.

The ultimate impact of tax incentives on learning can thus **vary greatly**, the more so because of the deadweight effect in some cases. The net result of this rather arbitrary and inconsistent application of tax policy to lifelong learning is to create mixed and inconsistent signals. Tax authorities in many countries remain reluctant to address the issue more systematically. There is now a need for education and finance ministries to take stock of the tax treatment of learning-related expenditure and revenues, evaluate its impact on investment in human capital, and consider whether policy needs to be adjusted.

The above points can be illustrated by reviewing current tax policy and recent developments in three countries. **In Austria**, there is widespread exemption of learning providers from VAT and many tax concessions exist for individuals and firms for certain categories of training expenditure. There has recently been a widening of eligible forms of learning for which individuals may claim income tax concessions. **In Finland**, revenue-side exemptions are limited to certain specified providers. The aim on the expenditure side is to favour all activities that contribute to people's future earning capacity. However this principle is hard to administer consistently. A commission established by the education authorities has clarified policy on expenditure by employers. **In the Netherlands**, the authorities have been particularly active in using tax policy to further the government's strong support for investment in human capital. Over the past decade they have introduced deductions to increase incentives for employers to invest in learning, to encourage training for particular target groups, and to encourage individuals to save for learning-related purposes. However, since 2002 fiscal pressures, doubts about the efficacy of some measures, and changing priorities have forced the government to cancel some of these initiatives.

Chapter 1

ALTERNATIVES TO UNIVERSITIES REVISITED

SUMMARY

A substantial portion of tertiary education is now provided outside universities, in institutions with a wide variety of characteristics. These institutions provide an alternative mechanism for expanding enrolments, and often offer better access and greater diversity than the traditional university. Many are vocational in orientation, but some offer leisure courses and some alternative routes into university study. While many focus on advanced study, others have courses at many levels. Non-university institutions sometimes emulate universities, but can also be distinctive in aims and methods. They are often less generously funded than universities, and this cannot always be justified by differences in programmes, raising important equity issues. While non-university institutions will have a clear role in future provision, their position and purpose within tertiary education systems are sometimes ambiguous. In these cases, countries need to resolve the distinctive purposes of such institutions, adapting structures and funding accordingly.

1. INTRODUCTION

In the past three decades, institutions providing tertiary education outside universities have become well-established features of OECD education systems. In a number of OECD countries (for example Canada, France, Germany, Ireland, New Zealand) institutions other than universities now account for a third or more of all tertiary enrolments and in a few (the Netherlands, Norway) they account for a majority (Table 1.1). There is a spectrum of such institutions: they can provide a broad mix of courses at both tertiary level and below; or they can teach primarily at the tertiary level. This chapter explores the purposes of such institutions, how they fit into the wider education system, and issues about funding, teaching quality, and economic outcomes. The chapter concludes by considering possible approaches to identity that these institutions might adopt, in building on present strengths to play a role in education systems of the future. It draws for illustrative purposes upon examples from OECD countries containing several different institutional models in order to shed light upon key policy issues.

When the OECD (1973) first examined non-university tertiary institutions three decades ago, in *Short-Cycle Higher Education: A Search for Identity*, they had yet to develop clear roles in most countries and were largely overshadowed by universities. Since then, their importance and size within education systems have grown dramatically. By 1991, when the OECD next examined them (OECD, 1991), they had become clear alternatives to universities within the tertiary landscape. The distinctive benefits they can offer include flexibility, high levels of equity and access, overtly vocational goals and a different approach to research and public service. At the same time, such institutions suffer from distinctive problems, in particular the challenge of finding roles and identities that make them attractive in competition with the higher-status university.

The development of this sector has come from two main sources. One is the need to expand tertiary education, in response to pressure from student aspirations and from the perception that in a knowledge-based economy more workers will need high-level skills (Grubb and Lazerson, 2004). Specifically, it has been argued in many countries that "higher-order" skills such as communication and problem-solving, as well as higher-level vocational skills beyond the end of secondary schooling, are necessary for a wider section of the population, a position the OECD has labelled "Tertiary Education for All" (OECD, 1998). Tertiary institutions outside universities can help enhance the supply of places for students, potentially at lower cost per student than universities and with fewer capacity constraints. And in some countries but not all, their lower tuition costs and their geographical proximity (with implications for lower housing costs), have attracted more students, potentially at the expense of university enrolments.

A second purpose for the development of a new sector has been to create a more diverse supply of tertiary education. Universities have at different times been criticised for being too rigid, too "academic" in the sense of detached from the real world, insufficiently interested in economic development and occupational preparation, too elitist, insufficiently concerned with teaching quality, too geographically remote and often too expensive. In some circumstances, such perceived shortcomings have led to the development of alternative institutions. For example, Germany's *Fachhochschulen* were established with a commitment to relationships with employers that universities lacked, while Norway's university colleges aim to provide more vocational and alternative forms of tertiary education. In other cases, such as further education colleges in the United Kingdom and TAFE (technical and further education) colleges in Australia, new tertiary provision has grown within institutions originally created (in many cases) to provide lower-level technical qualifications. Market forces have also played a role in increasing the growth of non-university tertiary institutions where they are more geographically accessible, often cheaper and can offer shorter and more applied courses than may be available in universities.

Figure 1.1 | Persons aged 15 and over participating in tertiary education by type of programme, 2001 (%)

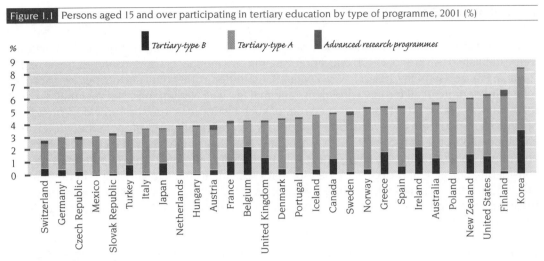

1. Advanced research programmes missing.

Source: OECD.

Data for Figure 1.1, p. 45.

Box 1.1 The definition of tertiary education

Tertiary education is traditionally defined not by where study takes place but by the characteristics of the course or programme. The accepted international classification of educational programmes, ISCED-97, distinguishes three types of tertiary programmes. OECD countries vary widely both in the overall size of their tertiary education systems, and in the share that each type of programme represents (see Figure 1.1).

ISCED 5A refers to programmes that are largely theoretically based and intended to provide sufficient qualifications for gaining entry into advanced research programmes and professions with high skills requirements. They are normally expected to be at least three years in duration, although examples exist of 5A programmes that are of shorter duration such as the university transfer programmes offered by Canadian and American community colleges.

ISCED 5B refers to programmes that, like ISCED 5A programmes, generally require successful completion of an upper secondary qualification or its equivalent for entry, but which are generally shorter, more practical, technical or occupationally specific than ISCED 5A programmes.

ISCED 6 refers to advanced research programmes, generally requiring submission of a thesis.

The boundary between 5A and 5B is in practice imprecise, as is the boundary between ISCED 5 and ISCED 4 – the latter referring to post-secondary programmes that are not considered to be tertiary level. See OECD (2004d) for more detailed definitions.

Box 1.1 defines the kind of programmes that are offered by tertiary institutions. Box 1.2 identifies the main examples of the institutions considered in this chapter. They vary greatly in terms of the distribution of students by level of study. Thus it should be borne in mind in interpreting this chapter that this sector is not homogeneous across countries. The expansion of non-university tertiary education has contributed to the heterogeneity of institutional types both within and across national education systems.

Table 1.1 Tertiary enrolments by type of programme and type of institution, 2001[1] (%)				
		Tertiary-type 5A enrolments (%)	Tertiary-type 5B enrolments (%)	Advanced research programme enrolments (%)	Total tertiary enrolments (%)
Australia (2002)	Universities	100	9	100	83
	TAFE	0	91	0	17
	Total	100	100	100	100
Austria (2001-02)	Universities	92	0	100	82
	Fachhochschulen	8	0	0	6
	Akademien	0	67	0	8
	Upper secondary vocational schools	0	33	0	4
	Total	100	100	100	100
Canada (1999-2000)	Universities	85	1	100	63
	Community colleges	15	99	0	37
	Total	100	100	100	100
Finland (2001-02)	Universities	55	0	100	57
	Polytechnics	45	0	0	42
	Other	<1	100	0	1
	Total	100	100	100	100
France (2001-02)	Universities	76	4	97	57
	Grandes écoles	13	1	3	6
	IUTs	0	24	0	9
	Other	11	71	0	28
	Total	100	100	100	100
Germany (2001-02)	Universities	75	0	m	64
	Fachhochschulen	25	0	m	21
	Other	0	100	m	15
	Total	100	100	100	100

Table 1.1 (continued) Tertiary enrolments by type of programme and type of institution, 2001[1] (%)					
		Tertiary-type 5A enrolments (%)	Tertiary-type 5B enrolments (%)	Advanced research programme enrolments (%)	Total tertiary enrolments (%)
Ireland (2001-02)	Universities	53	9	94	53
	Institutes of technology	17	80	2	38
	Other	8	11	4	9
	Total	100	100	100	100
Japan (2001)	Universities	100	0	100	75
	Junior colleges	0	32	0	8
	Colleges of technology	0	2	0	1
	Specialised training colleges	0	66	0	16
	Total	100	100	100	100
Netherlands (2002-03)	Universities	38	0	100	38
	Hogescholen	62	100	0	62
	Total	100	100	100	100
New Zealand (2002)	Universities	78	26	100	63
	Polytechnics	15	39	n	22
	Other	7	35	0	15
	Total	100	100	100	100
Norway (2002-03)	Universities	35	4	91	35
	University colleges	43	70	1	44
	Other	21	26	8	21
	Total	100	100	100	100

1. Or nearest year.

Notes:

Austria
University vocationally-oriented programmes and post-graduate courses of up to two years duration that are classified as ISCED 4C, 5B or 5A are currently not part of the tertiary education reporting system, and as a result enrolment data are missing. Enrolments in private universities such as business schools are not included.

Canada
Given the complexities involved in converting data to ISCED levels, matches to ISCED levels are only approximate. In community colleges 5B refers to programmes called "career technical". In universities 5B programmes are called "non-university programmes at university". 5A programmes in community colleges are "university transfer".

France
Tertiary-type 5A enrolments in "Other" institutions largely refer to the two-year *classes préparatoires* offered in *lycées* that prepare students for entry to a *grande école*. (As such they resemble the two-year Associate degree, or university transfer, programmes offered by Canadian and United States community colleges.) Tertiary-type 5B enrolments in "Other" institutions largely refer to the programmes leading to the *Brevet de technicien supérieur* qualification that are offered by the *Sections de techniciens supérieurs* within *lycées*.

Germany
Data on enrolments in advanced research (tertiary-type 6) programmes are not available, as data are recorded only at the point at which students apply for their degree. The institutions classified as "Other" offering tertiary-type 5B programmes include *Fachakademien* (specialised academies – Bavaria), *Schulen des Gesundheitswesens* (health sector schools), *Fachschulen* (trade and technical schools) and *Berufsakademien* (vocational academies).

Ireland
Refers to full-time equivalent enrolments. Universities include the National College of Art and Design. "Other" includes specialised institutions in areas such as hotel training, rural business development, the teaching of religion, theology, police training, and home economics teaching.

Netherlands
"Universities" include Open University enrolments but the number of students at the Open University includes only students who are studying for a tertiary qualification. Students who are only enrolled in short courses are excluded. ISCED 6 enrolments are for 2001. Enrolments in "Other" institutions are missing. A once-only 2001 survey indicated that there were some 60-70 such institutions, operating on a commercial basis, providing programmes at ISCED 5A and 5B. There were 29 000 students in programmes leading to tertiary qualifications in such institutions in 2001. This represented roughly 5% of total tertiary enrolments.

New Zealand
Refers to all students who have studied in a full year, but excludes private providers that receive no government funding. "Other" consists of: colleges of education; five institutions which specialise in teacher training; *wananga*, which are polytechnic-like institutions focused on programmes for Maori, the indigenous people of New Zealand; and private institutions.

Norway
"Other" tertiary institutions include: six specialised university-type institutions that offer programmes in a more limited number of fields than universities; two national institutes of the Arts; and private institutions.

Source: Data provided by national authorities.

2. PURPOSES

As Box 1.2 clarifies, those non-university institutions that provide tertiary education have taken shape in distinct patterns. The German-speaking countries have developed *Fachhochschulen* (FHS), starting in Germany in the late 1960s, although with differences among them. A different pattern, of developing technical institutes from clusters of vocational schools has occurred in Norway with its university colleges and in Finland with its polytechnics. The Dutch *Hogescholen* were also created out of secondary schools in 1986. In a third pattern, the English-speaking countries all have institutions offering a wide range of programmes only some of which are at tertiary level: community colleges in the United States and Canada, further education colleges in the United Kingdom, TAFE in Australia, polytechnics in New Zealand – as well as institutes of technology in Ireland. France, with its IUTs (*Instituts Universitaires de Technologie*), seems to be quite different from other countries in having developed an alternative to the traditional university within it but with a degree of legal autonomy from it.

The non-university institutions that provide tertiary education vary substantially in their purposes. As noted in the previous section, their rationale depends both on catering for an expanded tertiary education market and on serving a more diverse set of learning needs than has been provided for by universities. Yet the way they do so varies according to how they have evolved, in the differing institutional contexts of each country.

Box 1.2 **The non-university institutions that supply tertiary education**

Tertiary institutions are not classified by any standard international definitions, although the OECD (1991) has distinguished between universities and "alternatives to universities". As Figure 1.2 illustrates, they span a wide spectrum in their course profiles. They also differ widely in other respects: their missions, their funding, their governance structures. However in very broad terms they seem to fall into two groups, although the distinction is not absolute. On the one hand there are those which offer a wide mix of tertiary and non-tertiary programmes; and on the other there are those which predominantly offer tertiary programmes. The chapter refers principally to tertiary institutions in a limited number of countries, selected for illustrative purposes as examples of a wide range of models.

Institutions offering a broad mix of programmes

Australia's technical and further education (TAFE) colleges provide a wide mix of mainly short-duration qualifications for Australians of all ages (although the majority of students are adults): vocational courses, shorter upgrading courses, courses for the employees of specific firms, adult education, basic skills, and sometimes short-term labour market programmes. Although most students are not enrolled in tertiary courses, the colleges play a significant role in making ISCED 5B courses accessible. TAFE colleges were developed from the mid-1970s from former vocational and technical schools.

Canada's and the United States' community colleges offer a wide variety of vocational courses for new entrants, academic courses for students preparing for universities, shorter vocational courses for upgrade training, courses for the employees of specific firms, adult education, basic skills education, and sometimes short-term labour market programmes. As a result the variation in ages of their students tends to be wide.

Ireland's institutes of technology provide mainly short-duration tertiary qualifications (ISCED 5B), although also some courses at ISCED 5A and some at ISCED 4. Initially established in the 1970s mainly to teach engineering, science and business courses, they now cover a wide range of occupational fields, working closely with employers.

New Zealand's polytechnics offer a broad mix of tertiary and non-tertiary programmes. They provide a wide range of courses, from university-level degrees to secondary qualifications, and thus interact with both the university and the secondary school systems.

Other examples include further education colleges in the United Kingdom, which vary among England, Scotland, and Wales. Although all offer a mixture of tertiary and other levels of course, their orientation varies considerably. For example, about as many 16-to-19-year-olds studying for upper secondary qualifications in the United Kingdom are enrolled in further education colleges as in general secondary schools.

Institutions predominantly offering tertiary programmes

The following examples all award mainly ISCED 5A (degree-level) qualifications. Note that three-year or four-year courses at this level can still enhance flexibility compared to universities in some countries such as Germany and Austria where only longer-cycle first degrees have traditionally been available.

Austria's *Fachhochschulen* (universities of applied sciences) were developed from 1994 to offer three-year programmes with a strong labour market orientation.

...

Finland's polytechnics were established in 1991 by consolidating about 250 post-secondary vocational institutions. They are being used to achieve a major expansion in tertiary level participation.

France's *Instituts Universitaires de Technologie* (IUTs) were created in 1966 within the university system, but with shorter (two-year), more applied courses. In 2000 there were 101 IUTs within France's 86 universities.

Germany's *Fachhochschulen* were established in the late 1960s as three-year occupational programmes contrasted to the academic universities.

The Netherlands' *Hogescholen* were created from secondary schools in 1986, and form the most advanced part of a tiered system of vocationally-oriented education that starts at lower secondary level.

Norway's university colleges were created in 1994 by merging 98 smaller vocational colleges into 26 institutions, strengthening the provision of occupationally-oriented tertiary education.

Other examples include Swiss *Fachhochschulen* (OECD, 2003c), Flemish Belgium's *Hogescholen*, French Belgium's *Hautes Écoles*, and Japan's colleges of technology.

In some countries more than one type of institution provides tertiary education outside of the universities, but not all are discussed in this chapter. For example in France tertiary education is also provided in the two-year *classes préparatoires* offered in *lycées* to prepare students for entry to a *grande école*, as well as in programmes leading to the *Brevet de technicien supérieur* qualification that are offered by the *Sections de techniciens supérieurs* within *lycées*. In Germany, while the *Fachhochschulen* offer tertiary-type 5A programmes, tertiary-type 5B programmes are offered in institutions that include *Fachakademien* (specialised academies – Bavaria), *Schulen des Gesundheitswesens* (health sector schools), *Fachschulen* (trade and technical schools) and *Berufsakademien* (vocational academies).

Some institutions such as the German FHS and France's IUTs have a well-defined unitary purpose, concentrating on providing advanced-level (tertiary-type 5A) vocationally-oriented programmes closely linked to the demands of the labour market. Others can be described as multi-purpose. For example, community colleges in the United States provide a wide range of courses with academic and vocational purposes, some of which are designed to prepare students for future study. They also provide many week-end and evening courses, and serve functions as varied as upgrading basic literacy, allowing people to learn for leisure, and providing information and guidance about career and study choices. Like Australian TAFE colleges, but unlike most institutions with a well-defined unitary purpose, community colleges help serve the needs of "experimenters": students who are still exploring and developing their career interests (Grubb, 2002a, 2002b).

Three dimensions that help define the purposes of institutions are:

- The extent to which their goal is vocational preparation or a wider range of learning.

- The levels at which students are taught – in particular, the extent to which vocational preparation is oriented to basic or higher-order occupational skills.

- The extent to which institutions seek to serve their local communities, by widening access to tertiary study and/or engaging in locally-oriented research.

2.1. The extent of vocational orientation

The non-university institutions that offer tertiary education have in many countries been developed from older vocational institutions, often merging smaller colleges to create a more systematic set of institutions providing vocational preparation over a wide range of areas. They have mainly developed this way in Australia, Finland, the Netherlands, Norway and the United Kingdom and continue to be heavily vocational in their orientation, although in Norway this is gradually becoming less pronounced. Conversely, most community colleges in the United States and some in Canada were initially established in order to allow students to complete the first two years of a university degree, and academic study and transfer programmes remain important.

In Finland, Germany and Switzerland, non-university institutions have developed that are particularly focused on vocational preparation. Unlike universities they do not offer extensive general programmes in areas such as the humanities. Students are generally expected to go into employment immediately after completing a programme. Australia's TAFE colleges are similarly oriented, but do offer some general education courses that make up deficiencies in basic skills or prepare students for university entry. Community colleges in the United States and some community colleges in Canada commonly combine vocational programmes preparing students for employment and academic ones preparing them for university. An interesting variant is the French IUTs, which were founded with the unitary purpose of preparation for employment. However about 63% of IUT students now switch to universities after they complete the two-year course (HCEEE, 2003). This is helped by a common examination and qualifications ladder across tertiary institutions, which allows students to transfer after two years of study if they gain a qualification common to both IUTs and universities (the DEUG).

2.2. Levels of education provided

The institutions described in this chapter differ greatly in the level of education that they provide, as illustrated in Figure 1.2. This is partly a function of whether they are single or multiple purpose: North-American community colleges, for example, are places intended to serve a range of community needs from helping with basic literacy to advanced vocational preparation. However, even within the function of vocational preparation, the level varies.

Some institutions providing tertiary education also teach vocational skills at upper secondary school level (ISCED 3): for example building trades, clerical work and retail sales, car and engine repair, machining, metalwork, electrical applications and relatively low-level business and information technology. Such courses tend to be provided within upper secondary institutions in many European countries, and as part of apprenticeships in countries such as Austria, Germany and Switzerland. In English-speaking countries such as Australia, New Zealand and the United Kingdom, ISCED level 3 vocational programmes, although often with a lesser emphasis upon general education and generic skills than in countries such as Austria and Germany, are provided in specialised vocational institutions such as TAFE, further education colleges and polytechnics, with a dwindling number of such courses provided in the United States by community colleges.

The *Fachhochschulen* in Germany and Austria, the Norwegian university colleges, the *Hogescholen* in the Netherlands and the Finnish polytechnics provide almost entirely advanced programmes of three years or more – tertiary qualifications at ISCED level 5A. These are dominated by business, technology and communications courses; health occupations; sometimes social services and public administration; and in Norway also by teacher training. Such courses normally require an upper secondary qualification for entry, and the occupations that they prepare students for require significant reading and writing skills, and sometimes a substantial background in subjects such

| Figure 1.2 | Total enrolments in selected non-university tertiary institutions, by ISCED level,[1] 2001[2] (%) |

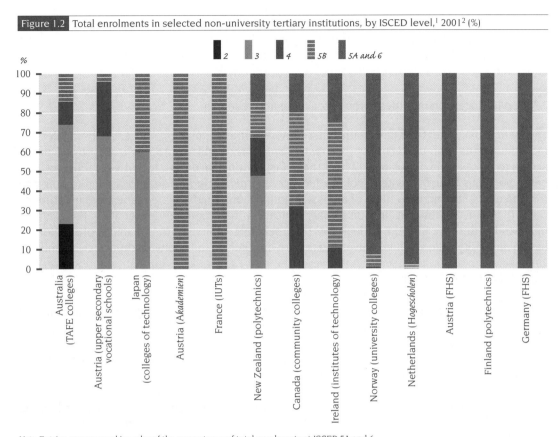

Note: Entries are arranged in order of the percentages of total enrolments at ISCED 5A and 6.

1. ISCED levels 4-6 are defined in Box 1.1. ISCED level 2 refers to lower secondary education, and ISCED level 3 to upper secondary education.

2. Or nearest year.

Source: OECD.

Data for Figure 1.2, p. 45.

as mathematics and science. These occupational areas tend to have equivalent programmes in universities, so transfer appears more natural. These kinds of knowledge-based occupations also represent 85% of occupational enrolments in United States community colleges. In many cases the occupations for which students are prepared are closer to professions than the older vocations of traditional upper secondary level vocational education and they include subjects such as business, health studies, information technology and engineering that are also offered by universities.

The level of occupational programmes offered by non-university institutions is in part a function of how the rest of the education system has developed. In countries with strong vocational education programmes within upper secondary education and with dual apprenticeship systems, such as Austria, Germany and Switzerland, institutions that provide tertiary education outside of the universities provide occupational programmes at a higher level, and often at a level (ISCED level 5A) equivalent to the programmes offered by universities. Where upper secondary vocational education is weaker, as in the United Kingdom and the United States, tertiary education outside of universities is provided within institutions that also provide lower level vocational preparation.

Traditionally, the image of vocational education has been dominated by older lower-status vocational programmes provided at the upper secondary level. This can influence the status of certain institutions that provide a wide range of qualifications, even though some of what they provide is at the more advanced tertiary level. If the image of these institutions could catch up with the reality of what they provide, it might give them somewhat higher status within tertiary education.

2.3. Serving local communities through teaching and research

The institutions other than universities that provide tertiary education are generally smaller and more numerous than universities. As a result, one of their clear purposes is to provide better access to more of the population. Where these institutions have been recently established, part of the point has been to create regional education centres, including ones located in remote and rural areas, which improve equity of access. In some countries there are many more institutions other than universities that provide tertiary education than there are universities. For example in Australia there are 87 TAFE colleges on 1 320 separate campuses but 37 universities; Norway has 26 university colleges but 4 universities plus 6 specialised university institutions; Finland has 20 universities but 31 polytechnics. (However the new *Fachhochshulen* in Austria and Switzerland are still not particularly numerous.)

In countries that have created these institutions from smaller specialised institutions, like Finland and Norway, they have been created to be more comprehensive in their offerings and to realise economies of scale, compared to the institutions they replaced. Therefore their scale reflects a compromise between these very small institutions and the much larger and less accessible universities, balancing accessibility against economies of scale.

There are several consequences of geographical proximity. In particular, access is easier, helping students of modest means to access tertiary education. And for some, particularly those with no tradition of higher education in their families, local institutions can be more attractive than distant universities that may be both unfamiliar and alienating. Moreover, such institutions serve public purposes roughly parallel to those of universities, focusing not on national research needs but more on local economic development and community needs. In many countries these institutions have been given responsibilities for local and regional research. For example, the Finnish polytechnics carry out research and development supporting polytechnic education itself as well as the working life of the region (OECD, 2003b). Regionally-related research and development is also characteristic of the German *Fachhochschulen*, which are responsible for research transfer into smaller and medium-sized enterprises and for working with public administration (Mayer, Mueller and Pollak, 2003). In France the most common research in the IUTs seems to be technical assistance to local enterprises. The act establishing university colleges in Norway specifically provided that they should engage in research connected to practice within specific occupational fields and to problems in their regions. Similarly, United States and Canadian community colleges carry out a variety of activities intended to enhance the local community, including advice to local firms (especially small- and medium-size enterprises) about new technologies, convening industry clusters and groups of local employers around common needs, identifying the education and technology needs of local employers, surveying the business environment for new developments and technologies, and helping attract new employers by providing customised training.

Such research can be hard to measure, partly because much of it is undertaken by individual staff independently of central monitoring (Grubb and Associates, 1999). In one attempt to quantify it, Kyvik and Skodvin (2003) estimated that about 20% of the time of academic staff in Norway's university colleges was spent on research and development, most of this (79%) on applied research and development rather than basic research. But many tertiary institutions that are much smaller than universities do not have the resources to develop much local research. As the 2003 OECD report on Swiss tertiary education noted, engagement by *Fachhoschulen* in applied research and research transfer remains "uneven" even though these institutions intend to increase their local research and development roles (OECD, 2003c).

The emergence of locally-oriented research and public service exemplifies a broader concept of research articulated by Boyer (1990) and Pratt (1997). They urged post-secondary institutions to move beyond the scholarship of discovery, which dominates the high-status research university, to include the scholarship of integration including synthesis and multi-disciplinary work; the scholarship of application including service to communities of practice; and the scholarship of teaching, in which staff carry out research on their own teaching. Many of the non-university institutions that offer tertiary education seem to be well-suited to the scholarship of application, including technology transfer, and to the scholarship of teaching. If the criteria for what constitutes serious research were broadened, then the status gulf between high-status research universities and tertiary colleges and institutes might become smaller.

2.4. Multiple purposes and the resulting trade-offs

In some countries, non-university tertiary institutions are created with multiple purposes. In others they acquire them through entrepreneurial drive, and through their greater openness to new markets compared to universities. In some cases, as in Australia and the United States, TAFE colleges and community colleges have created independent divisions to serve different purposes. These can provide courses that do not count toward a regular qualification, or self-supporting courses for hobbyists or the employees of specific firms. This pattern expands the scope of tertiary institutions beyond conventional academic and occupational preparation. It can also create synergies – for example, where the existence of occupational programmes creates research on local economic patterns – and complementarities, for example when an institution provides academic education that is also valuable in occupational programmes. Colleges with multiple missions are more likely to include courses and short programmes appropriate for older workers, particularly for the purposes of upgrade training, and therefore are more likely to serve the goals of lifelong learning. Finally, where students are uncertain about what subjects they want to pursue, the provision of both academic and occupational programmes makes the choices of educational pathways broader.

In addition, having many forms of education in one institution can be beneficial if institutions build educational bridges, or articulation mechanisms allowing students to move from one to another. For example, the community colleges in British Columbia and New Brunswick in Canada have created mechanisms to transfer adults from literacy programmes into the regular programmes. Some United States community colleges have created articulation mechanisms between lower-cost, more accessible non-credit programmes and credit programmes; and some community colleges have made it possible for students to count labour market programmes toward subsequent qualifications (OECD, 2001; Grubb, Badway and Bell, 2003).

However, the development of multiple purposes can come at a cost. If institutions try to do too many things, they may do none of them well. Further education colleges in the United Kingdom have been accused of failing to develop a clear purpose (Bailey, 2002), while complaints about "mission drift" and debates about priorities are common in United States community colleges (Bailey and Averianova, 1998). Even if institutions do retain quality across many areas, the image of a multi-purpose institution – somewhat like that of a department store with a very large number of offerings – may become diffuse and difficult to understand for students, employers and policy makers.

As the number of potential purposes expands, different colleges may emphasise one purpose over another, and so colleges within one sector start to vary. While such patterns may respond to local demand, they may also reflect institutional priorities that leave certain students' needs unmet.

Thus, having several forms of education available in one institution can have benefits but may prove counterproductive if taken too far. However, while legislative restriction is a policy option in keeping these institutions more narrowly focused, it also serves to restrict the entrepreneurial energy that is often seen as a desirable characteristic.

3. HOW INSTITUTIONS FIT INTO NATIONAL SYSTEMS OF EDUCATION AND TRAINING

A remarkable aspect of many of the institutions being considered in this chapter is how new they are. In Austria, Finland, Norway and Switzerland they are approximately a decade old; German *Fachhochschulen* are barely 30 years old, and France's IUTs not yet 40 years old. Even in countries where they were established relatively early, significant expansion is quite recent. In the United States community colleges first emerged in 1918, but they grew substantially only in the 1960s and 1970s. Australia's TAFE colleges originated in vocational and technical schools dating back to the beginning of the 20th century, though they took their present form and were greatly expanded after the mid 1970s. These are by and large relatively recent institutions, then, without encrusted traditions but with the problems of newness, particularly that of finding a distinctive role within national education systems.

3.1. Tiers of tertiary institutions

A common way to describe tertiary education systems has been to distinguish countries with a unitary system, with the great majority of enrolments concentrated in universities only, from those with a binary system, with universities and some type of non-university institutions (see, for example, Huisman and Kaiser, 2001). In such analyses, countries such as Sweden and Denmark are often regarded as having unitary systems. However such descriptions are rarely precise. For example Sweden has created advanced vocational training (*kvalificerad yrkesutbildning* or KY) courses which can be offered in several sectors: in municipal adult education state-funded vocational colleges, in private colleges, in labour market programmes for the unemployed, as well as in universities. Denmark, like Sweden, has large numbers of specialised providers of post-secondary education, and may be starting to consolidate some of them into technical institutes. This process might lead to the creation of a binary system (Kirsch, Beernaert and Norgaard, 2003, p. 99).

Norway with university colleges, Finland with polytechnics, and the Netherlands with *Hogescholen* can be described as binary systems. However, in many countries tertiary education is split into more than two parts, adding to the difficulty of cross-national comparisons. *Fachhochschulen* in Germany, Austria and Switzerland, for example, are not the only alternatives to universities. In Germany, as an example, the education system also includes *Fachschulen* (trade and technical schools) and *Berufsakademien* (vocational academies) which predominantly offer short duration (tertiary-type 5B) programmes. In Austria tertiary programmes are offered in *Akademien* and in upper secondary vocational schools, as well as in the universities and *Fachhochschulen*. Again, France offers an interesting variant, in which academic universities do not enjoy the highest status as places to study. *Grandes écoles* have the greatest prestige, with high spending per student and selective admissions, in contrast to universities, which must accept all students with the required qualification. The two-year IUTs also spend more per student than the universities, unlike the universities are able to select their students, and enjoy better teaching conditions. Offering a shorter route to completion, they are often preferred to universities (Foucade and Haas, 2002).

Moreover, distinctions between institutional categories may show only part of the picture, since important differences can also exist within a sector. For example, the English universities include both older universities and former polytechnics following the abolition of the divide between the two groups. In practice there are at least three segments of post-compulsory education. A group of universities that includes Oxbridge and the rest of the self-nominated Russell group of high-status universities (Barnett, 2003) sits alongside a second tier of universities, with lower levels of wealth and status, lesser research orientation, and more limited selectivity. The latter group includes the less prestigious older universities plus the newer universities that have been created from the former polytechnics. Further education colleges constitute a third group of institutions. They are consciously labelled *further* education and not *higher* education, and for most of their programmes, although not their tertiary programmes, they are funded through quite different mechanisms to the universities. Around 90% of the provision in further education colleges is below tertiary level. Australia has a comparable pattern, with a so-called "Group of Eight" high-status research-intensive universities, a second group of less prestigious universities, and TAFE colleges offering a relatively small set of programmes at tertiary level, in addition to a very large set of non-tertiary programmes. In the United States, a first tier of elite research universities is quite different in their selectivity, curricula, and completion rates from a second tier of less-selective and professionally-oriented universities – though tiers within the university system are hard to classify precisely, and analysts have suggested anything from three to ten sectors of tertiary education (Zemsky *et al.*, 1998).

Sometimes differences among categories or tiers of tertiary institutions are structured by policy (including funding policies and types of programmes allowed), and sometimes they reflect hotly-contested reputational differences creating fuzzy boundaries between first-tier and second-tier universities. The fact that some institutions are providing multiple levels of secondary and tertiary education adds to the complexity. However, one cannot escape the conclusion that different tiers of tertiary institutions enjoy different status, even where they are alternative suppliers of courses at a common level.

Recognising at least a tripartite structure explains why comparisons among countries are often so difficult. Community colleges are third tier institutions in the United States and Canada, and not directly comparable with the second-tier FHS in Germany, which aspire to be full universities. The university colleges in Norway are more comparable to the second-tier FHS or polytechnics in Finland, and have less in common with TAFE or further education colleges. Some less-selective and second-tier universities in the United States and the United Kingdom are heavily occupational or professional, and seem more like the occupationally-oriented FHS, Norwegian university colleges, and Finnish polytechnics. This tripartite structure also helps explain why the international ISCED classification of courses (see Box 1.1) is often awkward. These levels also matter because they are related to other differences among institutions, like the levels of occupational programmes they offer.

3.2. Enrolment shares and targets

In terms of volume, enrolments in institutions other than universities now occupy an important place in many countries' tertiary education systems. For a number of countries, Table 1.1 estimates the share of tertiary 5A, 5B and 6 enrolments, and of total tertiary enrolments, accounted for by universities and by non-university tertiary institutions. Figure 1.2 provides information on the distribution across all ISCED categories of enrolments in selected non-university tertiary institutions. It is clear that countries differ greatly both in the overall share of total enrolments accounted for by non-university institutions, and in the share at each ISCED level contained within non-university institutions. Non-university institutions have fewer than one in five tertiary enrolments in Australia and Austria, but nearly two thirds in Norway and the Netherlands. In

Finland and Ireland, non-university institutions account for around half of all tertiary enrolments. In sheer size alone tertiary institutes and colleges now occupy an important place in post-secondary education.

Several countries aim to increase non-university institutions' share of total tertiary enrolments. Germany hopes to have 40% of enrolments in *Fachhochschulen*, though universities have opposed this; Austria hopes that its *Fachhochschulen* will be able to provide for a third of new students; and Finland plans to expand tertiary education to admit 70% of the youth cohort, with all expansion in the polytechnics. The United Kingdom has a target of 50% of the relevant age group enrolled in higher education by 2010, and many observers think a great deal of this growth will come in tertiary-level courses provided by further education colleges. A cautious prediction might be that non-university institutions will continue to increase as a fraction of tertiary education for reasons of cost, proximity, economic focus, and variety. However, the expansion of tertiary education in universities versus the various alternatives is clearly one of the important policy questions that countries face.

3.3. Linkages to other parts of the system

Students progressing from secondary into tertiary education, and from one form of tertiary education to another, can often benefit from linkages between different levels of learning. Such linkages can help prepare and orient students for such transitions. One potential advantage of institutions that offer programmes at several levels is that they can create pathways or bridges among different kinds of study. For example, an individual in a short labour market programme could potentially transfer into the mainstream of tertiary education, though this route has not been well developed in any country; someone needing basic skills can continue in vocational programmes; and individuals in adult education programmes may find that they can then return for a tertiary-level programme to upgrade their employment. Potential linkages may be affected substantially by public policies, particularly those that link (or fail to link) non-university tertiary institutions with universities and that promote or hinder competition with adult education.

Universities

Non-university tertiary institutions vary in the extent to which they are linked to or integrated with universities and other sectors of the education system. Course profiles are one aspect of this. Table 1.1, which draws for illustrative purposes upon data from a limited number of OECD countries, shows a range of patterns:

- In some countries (for example Austria) most tertiary-type 5A programmes are provided in universities and most type 5B programmes in non-university institutions.

- In others such as Norway there is a more or less even spread of 5A across alternative providers.

- In New Zealand both universities and other institutions are involved in both type 5A and type 5B provision.

Another distinguishing feature of non-university tertiary institutions revealed by Table 1.1 is that, almost without exception, they provide very few of advanced research programmes (ISCED 6).

Many of the non-university institutions that offer tertiary education are integrated with universities to some extent. For example in the United States and in parts of Canada, the function of transferring students to universities is symbolically important for tying community colleges to higher education. However, there are frequent complaints that transfer rates are too low, and a great deal of controversy about whether universities or the colleges are to blame. In a different pattern, France's IUTs were created to provide occupational preparation at tertiary level rather than access to university. However, many students (as many as 63%) who complete the two-year programme then go on to university because of the higher status and employment benefits of its degree (HCEEE, 2003). The fact that IUTs are part of particular universities facilitates such movement. In the United Kingdom local further education colleges often create articulation arrangements with local universities, even though there is nominally a rigid divide between *further* education and *higher* education.

While almost all countries allow transfer in some way, in practice there are barriers to transfer that are sometimes institutional, sometimes personal (for example, when students cannot afford to stay in education), and sometimes locational (when tertiary colleges are located a considerable distance from universities). Transfer rates therefore vary substantially within as well as among countries, for reasons that need closer investigation.

Upper secondary institutions

A second kind of linkage involves connections to secondary schools. Some institutions, such as community colleges in the United States, have become concerned about the competence of entering students. In response, they have created a wide variety of articulation mechanisms with secondary schools, some intended to improve the quality of preparation and others smoothing the transition between secondary and post-secondary education (Orr, 2002). But in some countries, such as Australia and the United Kingdom, the non-university institutions that provide tertiary education themselves provide a significant proportion of programmes at upper secondary (ISCED 3) level. In this context secondary schools and the institutions that are the focus of this chapter may compete rather than co-operate. In England, national policy has stimulated competition in the provision of post-16 education, and further education colleges compete with secondary schools to provide preparation for upper secondary exams as well as other vocational qualifications.

Labour market programmes

A third area of potential linkages involves short-term labour market programmes, intended to help unemployed people return to work. These are often similar to some courses offered in institutions that also offer tertiary programmes. For example, some labour market programmes offer preparation in computer skills and information technology, in basic business practices, and in lower-level health occupations just as the institutions that also offer tertiary programmes do. For this reason, in the United States as well as in other countries, labour market programmes have in the past subcontracted with community colleges or similar institutions to provide training. Potentially this offers opportunities to transfer between the short labour market programmes and longer programmes, providing routes into tertiary study. In other countries such linkages have been comparatively rare. In Austria, for example, the *Fachhochschulen* concentrate on their three-year programmes, and rarely bid to provide short labour market programmes (OECD, 2004a). In general, opportunities to create these types of articulated pathway seem to be greater where a single institution offers programmes at several educational levels.

Adult education

A fourth possible linkage is to programmes designated as adult education. Adult education encompasses a broad range of provision (OECD, 2003a), from the kinds of programmes for adults provided in technical colleges and universities to a vast range of informal courses provided by non-governmental organisations. Non-university tertiary institutions have been more active in adult education than in the provision of labour market programmes. The *Fachhochschulen* in Austria, for example, have created evening programmes intended for working students, as have the Finnish polytechnics (OECD, 2003b), although the scale of the provision remains relatively small compared to programmes provided for younger students. Further education, TAFE, and community colleges in the English-speaking countries provide large amounts of evening and week-end courses targeted at working adults, and are among the largest providers of this form of adult education. Some community colleges in Canada have established community-based centres that provide adult education, which can then be linked to other courses at the colleges. United States community colleges have done the same in community-based divisions offering courses that do not provide credit towards formal qualifications, but may prepare students to enter credit-bearing programmes.

In contrast, in several countries the non-university institutions that predominantly offer tertiary programmes tend to operate on conventional schedules of day- and week-time classes, and with relatively fewer older students. Table 1.2 compares for five countries the age distribution of university and non-university students who are in tertiary-type 5A courses. In each country it is striking to what extent universities tend to enrol fewer young students and more adults compared to their non-university counterparts.

Table 1.2 Age distribution of ISCED 5A enrolments by type of institution, 2001[1]

	Institution	<24	25-34	35+	Total
			Age distribution		
Austria	Universities	52.3	37.6	10.2	100.0
	FHS	65.4	27.8	6.8	100.0
Finland	Universities	45.7	38.2	16.2	100.0
	Polytechnics	60.8	27.1	12.1	100.0
Germany	Universities	47.8	42.1	10.2	100.0
	FHS	48.8	44.0	7.2	100.0
Netherlands	Universities	68.1	22.7	9.2	100.0
	Hogescholen	74.1	16.7	9.2	100.0
Norway	Universities	47.3	38.6	14.0	100.0
	University colleges	41.4	30.2	28.4	100.0

1. Or nearest year.

Source: National authorities.

4. THE DILEMMAS OF FUNDING

Expansion of tertiary education has placed new strains on funding in many countries. Overall costs can rise not just with student numbers but also with an upgrading in the educational content of programmes, as for example occurred in Norwegian university colleges and the Finnish polytechnics, or because the courses that are offered require more expensive equipment and workshops. (Potentially, this can be offset if a country substitutes lower-cost tertiary institutions for higher-cost universities.) At least three other issues arise from this starting point: the level of funding; student contributions; and the overall structure of funding.

4.1. At what level are non-university tertiary institutions funded?

In most countries, non-university tertiary institutions are being used to expand tertiary education at lower cost per student than expanding universities. For example:

- Past comparisons between per-student spending in those non-university institutions that largely offer tertiary programmes on the one hand and universities on the other have shown spending in the former to be 46% less in Germany (in 1995: Scheuer and Schmidt, 2000), 18% less in Norway (in 1997: Norwegian Social Science Data Services, 1997) and 16% less in Finland (in 2000: OECD, 2003b).

- In the United States, with greater inequalities than most OECD countries, spending per full-time equivalent student averaged $7 665 in community colleges in 2000, compared to $11 345 in public universities granting master's degrees, $17 780 in public doctoral institutions, and $32 512 in research universities (NCES, 2002, Table 342).

- France is an exception since IUTs spent one third *more* per student than universities, in 2001, although this annual per-student difference still means a two-year IUT course costs less than a university degree (ministère de l'Éducation nationale, de l'Enseignement supérieur et de la Recherche, 2002).

Insufficient attention has been paid to *why* non-university institutions spend less per student than do universities. Of course, they do not support research and post-graduate (tertiary-type 6) education to the same extent as universities, as Table 1.1 and Figure 1.2 make clear, and the costs associated with staff are typically lower, potentially contributing to lower-quality faculty and more turnover. Student services also appear to be funded at lower levels, at least in English-speaking countries. This is less clearly the case in the German-speaking countries, where the *Fachhochschulen* have status equivalent to universities, or in France, where IUT students have access to the facilities of the universities to which they are affiliated. But present data do not give a full account of what lies behind the differences – for example, the extent to which facilities are more crowded.

The differentials in spending between non-university institutions and universities are part of a structure of inequality resulting from the differentiation of tertiary institutions (Grubb and Lazerson, 2004). Of course, institutions providing different programmes may legitimately spend different amounts per student – especially if they offer high-cost programmes requiring expensive equipment and laboratories. But the differences in most countries between spending on universities and on non-university alternatives are larger and more systematic than differences in programmes can explain. From a policy perspective, expanding tertiary education through non-university institutions is cheaper than expansion in universities, and may therefore appear more efficient. From the perspective of students, however, lower levels of funding may also mean institutions with larger classes, less contact with teaching staff, potentially lower-quality staff, fewer student services, less adequate physical facilities, and potentially lower completion rates. To the extent that these disadvantages arise, using lower-cost institutions to expand tertiary provision may have a double-edged effect on equity. The benefit of tertiary education may spread to a wider section of the population. However new inequities within tertiary provision may lead to less advantaged students being more likely to participate in less generously funded institutions, and to have more limited educational aspirations than they might have if they were drawn into universities. In the United States, this has led to a debate about whether community colleges *increase* education for some individuals who would otherwise not have gone beyond secondary school ("educational upgrading"), or whether they *decrease* education for individuals who might otherwise have gone to university ("cooling out"). While there is now fairly conclusive empirical evidence that upgrading dominates cooling out (Dougherty, 1994; Grubb, 1996; Rouse, 1995 and 1998), the debates clarify that equity issues in tertiary colleges are more difficult than they appear at first glance. They involve such issues as proximity, tuition levels, guidance and counselling, and student support services. In light of such considerations, Norway has recently introduced a new system of financing in which differences in funding between types of institutions will gradually be reduced.

4.2. How much should students contribute?

The relative costs to students of different kinds of tertiary education tend to divide into two patterns. In United States and Canadian community colleges, tuition costs are much lower than those in universities. While there is considerable variation among states and provinces, public university tuition costs are typically several thousand dollars while community college tuition costs in the United States were under one thousand in the late 1990s (Zemsky *et al.*, 1998). In Canada currently they are around two thousand dollars. Similarly in Australia, courses in TAFE colleges cost students a great deal less than do university courses. As a result, students earning a tertiary qualification through TAFE end up paying less overall than those who enter a university. These cost differentials, along with lower living costs associated with proximity, could help explain the differences in growth rates among these institutions.

In other countries, however, tuition costs do not differ across institutions – in Scandinavian countries because tertiary education has been free for all students, and in Austria and Switzerland because the costs of *Fachhochschulen* and universities are the same, and relatively modest compared to tuition costs in countries like the United States. In such cases, tuition differentials cannot explain patterns of enrolment growth.

However, many countries are starting to rethink policies of zero or low tuition costs, precisely because the increasing costs of tertiary education are starting to outrun available revenues. In parts of the United Kingdom there are recent proposals that universities be allowed to increase tuition fees up to £3 000, potentially expanding the differential cost of universities versus further education colleges. Similarly, problems in financing tertiary education and the evident unfairness of high subsidies to middle- and upper-income students in universities have weakened the taboo on discussing tuition in some Scandinavian countries (OECD, 2003b). If pressures for expanding tertiary education continue to increase, tuition cost differentials might grow in other countries, reflecting the actual difference in the cost of providing courses. If this were the case, then patterns of attendance such as those observed in the United States might also develop, where students take the first few years of tertiary education in community colleges because of lower fees, and then transfer to universities.

Of course, tuition costs may be offset by access to grants, loans, or tax credits. In a number of countries non-university institutions have been at a disadvantage in access to these funds. In Australia, for example, the Higher Education Contribution Scheme – in which students repay loans for university out of future income – is unavailable to TAFE students (although the costs of tuition and post-graduation earnings are also lower). In the United States, eligible community college students are much less likely to get either grants or loans than are comparable university students (Grubb and Tuma, 1991). This can result in the short-term costs to students of community colleges courses being higher than university courses.

In considering what a national approach to funding tertiary education ought to accomplish, it may in principle be possible to set a criterion of neutrality between institutions: setting tuition costs, grants and loans so that students from all income levels are equally encouraged to attend tertiary education, unbiased between non-university institutions and universities. Such a principle, might, however, require income-contingent tuition costs (or income-adjusted grants and loans), and perhaps tuition cost differentials favouring non-university tertiary institutions (Gallagher, 2003).

Until countries recognise the complexities in funding a more complex system of tertiary education, these funding differences and the student reactions they cause will remain potential problems.

4.3. How should funding be structured overall?

Tertiary institutions may receive funding from different levels of government, from students, from employers and potentially from research funds. In some countries like Austria and Norway, non-university tertiary institutions are creations of the national government, funded by national revenues on a level basis. In federal countries like Australia and Switzerland, they are legally the responsibility of states or provinces. Where their funding derives mostly from states or provinces rather than central government their revenues may be unequal across the country, especially in the United States and Canada where state and provincial incomes vary widely. Moreover, where non-university tertiary institutions are clearly local in their mission, serving the local economy, local funding is important. Examples include community colleges in some states of the United States and in some Canadian provinces, and polytechnics in Finland, where 43% of funding comes from municipal governments. Municipal funding may enhance responsiveness to local conditions and demands, but may add to inequalities between richer and poorer areas. Grants from either provincial or national levels could even out such inequalities, though such mechanisms have not generally been a priority.

While employers may benefit from a better-educated local workforce, employer contributions to the cost of institutions are not widely used. Exceptions include fees paid by employers for firm-specific training on a fee-for-service basis, as in United States and Canadian community colleges, Australian TAFE colleges and Austrian FHS. Another model is an employer tax to support vocational training, like the one in Quebec, Canada, where employers who do not provide training must contribute to a tax fund for training. Such a tax might support continuing education in tertiary institutes, though there is little evidence that this takes place in Quebec (OECD, 2004b).

A few countries have separate funding for research or for local service. In the United States, for example, many states fund training for local companies through community colleges. Several countries have earmarked funds for local research and public service. In the absence of explicit funding, the extent of such activities appears to be uneven and idiosyncratic, and it is difficult to learn how much of it goes on.

Finally, Finland has established some performance-based funding, based on evaluations of excellence in teaching, excellence in regional impact, and general performance criteria including completion rates. The United Kingdom also has some performance-based funding, since some fraction of payment to further education colleges depends on students completing programmes. In 2002 Norway introduced performance-based funding for both teaching and research, with a common funding structure for universities and university colleges. However performance-based funding is not yet widespread in those non-university institutions in which tertiary education is provided.

There is no single ideal funding structure for non-university tertiary institutions. However, any approach needs clear answers to a series of questions:

- Are these institutions sufficiently like universities to merit a common funding structure? For some tertiary institutes such as Germany's *Fachhochschulen* where teaching profiles and qualification levels resemble those of universities, differences in funding may be hard to defend. But in some cases governments may recognise that non-university institutions need different funding mechanisms to serve different students and different goals, to serve local purposes, and to remain flexible and responsive.

• How should the burden of funding be spread among beneficiaries, including students, employers, and different levels of government? Under benefit taxation and pricing, for example, students might pay for tuition according to the economic benefits they receive, employers might contribute via taxation, and the government would contribute based on the estimated public benefits of education. However, such approaches are generally modified by the histories and values associated with tertiary education, since in some countries it has been unthinkable either to charge for tuition or to tax employers.

• Can inequitable funding among tertiary institutions of different types be removed (for example through tuition, grant, and loan schemes aiming to enhance equity among students)?

• How can funding reflect the various specific goals of institutions? Could separate funding streams for particular purposes – for example local research, student services, firm-specific training and perhaps lifelong learning as distinct from pre-employment education – ensure that some goals are explicitly supported?

Deliberations about alternative funding mechanisms might help countries to continue expanding the resources for alternatives to universities while assuring that their multiple purposes are well-served.

5. THE QUALITY OF TEACHING

Universities have often been accused of having poor teaching, dominated by lectures, in large classes with little interaction among students and professors, with dry academic content and few applications (see for example: Mayer, Mueller and Pollak [2003] for Germany; Eurydice [2000] for France; Grubb and Associates [1999] for the United States; and Harkin and Davis [1996a and 1996b] for England). In countries such as Finland and France the low quality of university teaching has been an explicit reason for establishing alternatives. The hope has been that different institutions can create new cultures around teaching to facilitate more student-centred approaches, more applied teaching, more inter-disciplinary teaching, greater use of new technology, and greater respect for vocational subjects. In the United States community colleges pride themselves on being "teaching colleges", with smaller classes. In the United Kingdom further education college instructors say that they favour student-centred approaches (Grubb and Associates, 1999; Harkin and Davis, 1996a and 1996b).

However, the potential for changing teaching practice is not always realised. In Germany, for example, both universities and the *Fachhochschulen* have been accused of "structural neglect" in the quality of teaching: they seem to have developed similar approaches to teaching as universities (Mayer, Mueller and Pollak, 2003). In the United Kingdom, Harkin and Davis (1996a and 1996b) found that while many instructors claim to use discussion and small-group techniques, most teaching remained dominated by lecture methods. In the United States, instruction in community colleges most often follows the lecture format, although individual instructors may teach in novel ways and a few colleges have developed institutional mechanisms to improve teaching more generally (Grubb and Associates, 1999).

A further problem affects teaching in vocational subjects, which dominate courses in non-university tertiary institutions. These subjects usually include workshops or laboratories, and teaching staff face the task of integrating classroom instruction and practice-oriented instruction. Vocational teaching often requires complex competences: many occupations (for example architecture, drafting) require visual competences; some (the conventional trades, technical occupations, some health fields) require manual skills; many require sophisticated interpersonal abilities such as co-operation and communication; and many occupations require applied and non-standard forms of reading, writing, mathematics, and other general education subjects. Vocational instructors must balance the needs of different constituents: students interested in acquiring competences for the long term; employers with demands for short-run performance; and often licensing mechanisms and examinations for qualifications. But while there has been extensive attention to the teaching of reading, writing, and mathematics, there has in most cases not been comparable attention to teaching in business, technical fields, health occupations, or other vocational areas except in the German tradition (Achtenhagen and Grubb, 2001). So vocational teaching, in many ways more difficult than academic teaching, has fewer sources of information and support.

In the current writing on non-university institutions that offer tertiary programmes, there has been strikingly little attention to instructional issues. One looks in vain for any references to the nature of instruction in any of the prior OECD reports, or the series of country reports by Eurydice entitled "Two Decades of Reform in Higher Education in Europe: 1980 Onwards", or comparative work like Huisman and Kaiser (2001) or Kirsch, Beernaert and Norgaard (2003). If tertiary colleges and alternative universities are to realise their potential for improving teaching compared to universities, then they will need to direct more attention to the many ways of promoting innovation in teaching.

6. ECONOMIC BENEFITS

Tertiary education can provide a wide variety of potential benefits, including increases in knowledge of many different sorts, greater sophistication and precision in thinking, changes in values like tolerance and receptivity to new ideas, greater familiarity with the range of human accomplishments and the humanities, greater willingness to engage in political and civic life, as well as the degrees and qualifications that gain access to better employment and higher earnings (Schuller *et al.*, 2003). However, most of the non-university institutions that offer tertiary education are oriented primarily towards occupational purposes: they pursue economic benefits for students, employers and the economy.

Such benefits are not always easy to measure. In many countries – like Austria, Finland, Norway and Switzerland – the newer types of tertiary institutions are too new to have been extensively evaluated. In other countries with more extensive histories, much information about economic benefits is anecdotal, for want of appropriate data. As a result, benefits are often taken as an article of faith, rather than resting on a firm empirical base.

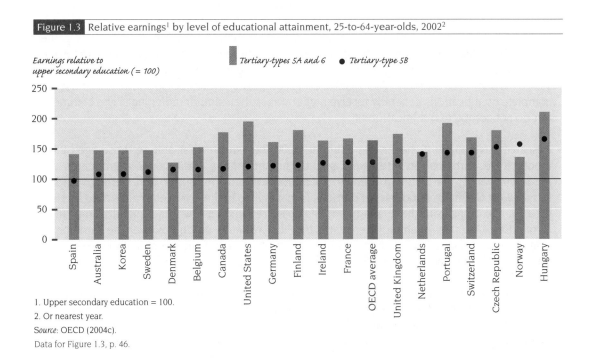

Figure 1.3 Relative earnings[1] by level of educational attainment, 25-to-64-year-olds, 2002[2]

1. Upper secondary education = 100.
2. Or nearest year.
Source: OECD (2004c).
Data for Figure 1.3, p. 46.

One indicator of economic benefits is the earnings pattern associated with tertiary-type 5A and 5B programmes. There is not a precise match between these ISCED classifications and tertiary institutions (as Table 1.1 clarified). And in countries such as Norway where tertiary-type 5B programmes are a quite small proportion of total tertiary enrolments the estimates may be based upon small sample sizes. Nevertheless it is still the best available data. Figure 1.3 shows the earnings of individuals who have completed tertiary-type 5A and 5B programmes, relative to the earnings of individuals with upper secondary education only. In 2002 in the 19 countries for which data are available, adults with tertiary-type 5B qualifications earned on average 26% more than those with just upper secondary qualifications. This premium ranged from 10% or less in Australia, Korea, Spain and Sweden to over 50% in the Czech Republic, Hungary and Norway. These benefits are substantially less than those that flow from tertiary-type 5A qualifications: adults at this level earn on average 64% more than upper secondary graduates. This suggests why the university remains such a powerful attraction: while the qualifications that are awarded by non-university institutions appear to result in substantial economic benefits, they are not as large as those from universities.

Where, as in the case of Germany's FHS or Finland's polytechnics, non-university institutions generally offer the same level of qualification as the universities (both tertiary-type 5A) the data shown in Figure 1.3 provide little guidance on the economic benefits that non-university institutions provide for tertiary graduates. In such cases national data provide a better guide. Fortunately a number of countries have accumulated evidence allowing more detailed conclusions to be drawn:

• In the United Kingdom, males with sub-degree qualifications earn an average of 14% more than those with secondary qualifications; it is 18% more for females. The first university degree earns an additional 10% for males and 26% for females. However, the returns from specific kinds of qualifications vary enormously: some low-level qualifications (NVQs) have negative effects while others have benefits as high as 22% for men and almost 36% for women (Dearden *et al.*, 2000). Such results clarify the importance of looking at the particular types of qualifications when non-university institutions offer a wide variety of programmes.

• In Australia, the results indicate a relatively modest benefit from tertiary credentials gained from TAFE colleges. For example males who have completed an Associate Diploma (a tertiary-type 5B qualification) earn 9% more than those who have completed only upper secondary school, and females 8% more (Ryan, 2002a and 2002b). The evidence also shows that those who complete qualifications generally receive higher wages than similar individuals who commence but do not complete qualifications.

• Research in Germany (Scheuer and Schmidt, 2000) has shown that among those aged 25-54, labour force participation rates were slightly higher among *Fachhochschulen* graduates than among university graduates in the 1991-97 period in both the former East Germany and the former West Germany. Labour force participation was also higher for both groups than for those with qualifications from the dual apprenticeship system or those with no qualifications. In the former East Germany unemployment rates for *Fachhochschulen* graduates over the same period were generally slightly higher than for university graduates, but they were slightly lower in the former West Germany.

• Research on community colleges in the United States indicates substantial benefits from completing two-year degrees, of the order of 20% for men and 30% for women compared to completing only upper secondary school. These are smaller than the returns to a university degree, but community college qualifications require only half as much time to complete. Not surprisingly, there are substantial differences among fields of study, with the economic benefits particularly high for business, for technical occupations, and for health occupations (especially nursing for women) and low in agriculture and early childhood programmes. In addition, the earnings effects of community colleges (and universities as well) are much higher for those who find employment related to their field of study, especially for women. The data also show that students who complete small amounts of education in community colleges, failing to complete a qualification, are unlikely to benefit from it (Grubb, 2002a).

- Similarly, French data indicate that individuals who started a two-year credential in an IUT but failed to complete it suffer an earnings penalty of about 15% compared to those who complete the credential (Giret, Moullet and Thomas, 2002; Cereq, 2003).

The dependence of outcomes on completing courses is significant. Rates of completing qualifications are often unknown because of the lack of longitudinal data (OECD, 2003a). However, there are widespread concerns that completion rates are lower in non-university providers of tertiary education than they should be. For example, in Germany there is general concern that non-completion has increased because of problems in the transition between secondary and tertiary institutions, with rates of non-completion thought to be 30% in universities and 22% in *Fachhochschulen* (Mayer, Mueller and Pollak, 2003). Finland has reported that 7% of students drop out of polytechnics each year, implying perhaps a 28% dropout rate over a four-year course (OECD, 2003b). Of United States students entering community colleges in 1995-96, 36% earned some credential within five years, 47% were not enrolled five years later and had no credential, while 18% were still studying (Berkner *et al.*, 2002). Interview results indicate that high non-completion among older students is often due to the "family-work-schooling dilemma" where students with families and employment responsibilities leave education if their schedules become too complex (Gittell and Steffy, 2000; Matus-Grossman and Gooden, 2002; Woodlief, Thomas and Orozco, 2003).

This evidence on economic benefits, though incomplete, shows that non-university institutions that offer tertiary education can generate substantial returns, but that these cannot be automatically assumed. Benefits vary by length and type of programme, by field of study, by gender, by whether individuals are employed in their field of study, and by whether they complete courses. A more thorough understanding of the nature and magnitude of these benefits requires better data.

7. CONCLUSION

A substantial amount of tertiary education now takes place in institutions outside universities, and the institutions that provide this have become well established within tertiary provision. However, success and sheer size do not by themselves resolve the problems of identity. As with everything else in tertiary education there is enormous variation among countries and within countries, so that blanket generalisations are difficult. However, institutions have developed at least four approaches to defining their roles:

- In some countries, non-university institutions aspire to become or emulate universities, and they spend a great deal of institutional and political energy trying to do so. In Norway, some of the university colleges aspire to become full universities awarding the master's degree and some doctoral degrees: a 2002 amendment to the relevant Act makes formal upgrading to university status possible. In Germany there is keen competition by the *Fachhochschulen* to gain university status, and they are trying to establish parity with universities in salaries of faculty, hours of teaching, civil service grades of faculty, and access to research (Mayer, Mueller and Pollak, 2003). Some community colleges in the United States have successfully become degree-granting institutions, as have a small number of Australian TAFE colleges. Universities often resist such moves, and such opposition partly explains the inability in Germany to meet the target of 40% of tertiary students in *Fachhochschulen* (Table 1.1 indicates that the proportion is now only 21%). In Finland universities have resisted (although unsuccessfully) a role for polytechnics in research, as well as their proposal to offer master's programmes.

While upgrading their status makes sense for individual institutions, some benefits of a differentiated tertiary education system may be lost. Policy makers may potentially resist this trend by using carrots such as rewards for teaching well or funding for applied research, as well as sticks like governance mechanisms, restriction of funding to non-degree students, regulation of which qualifications an institution can provide, and specification of staff credentials.

- A second approach is for non-university institutions to collaborate with universities, for example by offering joint qualifications or clear pathways into universities, rather than to compete with them. In Canada, particularly British Columbia, some community colleges now offer four-year degrees in conjunction with local universities, allowing them to be called "university community colleges". In countries such as Australia and England national policies have acted to maintain a strong distinction between universities and non-university institutions. However, in practice some non-university institutions in both countries participate in higher education by offering the first one or two years of university-level coursework, and then articulating with local universities. In England others provide full degree courses accredited by collaborating universities. In Flemish Belgium, as a result of the Bologna Process to harmonise European tertiary qualifications, the Higher Education Act stipulates formal co-operation between a university and one or more *Hogescholen*. This will help to create bridges between the bachelor's and master's levels. In less formal ways, some community colleges in the United States have established articulation agreements with local universities so that transfer becomes all but automatic, and a college may then become known as a feeder school into a university.

- A third tactic has been to abandon the drive to become universities where it is perceived that the battle cannot be won in competition for status with long-established universities. A clear alternative has been to develop into a local or regional institution that is distinctive from universities: more flexible; more responsive to local conditions including local labour market conditions; better at providing a wide range of programmes including lifelong learning for adults, training for employers, labour market programmes, and adult or non-vocational education as well as conventional pre-employment preparation; better at moving research into practice including technology transfer; better at public service to local employers and governments; and better able to participate in local economic development. The attempt to develop comprehensive regional centres is characteristic of some Norwegian university colleges, the Finnish polytechnics for which a distinctive approach to tertiary education has been central, and the more comprehensive community colleges in the United States and Canada. By devising an alternative model to the university, these institutions can escape competition with better-established institutions. They can define their own conceptions of institutional excellence, rather than relying on conceptions defined by others; and they can become special parts of tertiary education rather than university look-alikes.

- In a fourth pattern, some non-university institutions have remained substantial providers of vocational education at sub-tertiary level, including a range of short courses and programmes. Among the institutions examined in this chapter, the Australian TAFE colleges best fit this pattern. Their catalogues provide an enormous range of courses, including many that would be provided in upper secondary schools in other countries, and most students are part-time, attending for only a few hours per week. This strategy creates a very different kind of institution than one providing largely full-time tertiary-type 5A courses, in which students may also be involved in a range of extra-curricular activities that help develop their interests and identities.

In institutions such as TAFE colleges, students typically come for coursework and then leave, and rarely take coursework unrelated to their qualification or engage in other student activities. Funding mechanisms encourage this: colleges are paid for student enrolments in programmes leading to qualifications, and they receive little institutional funding that might support the broader activities of other types of educational institutions.

These strategies are not mutually exclusive, and some institutions have developed a hybrid approach, allowing some students to treat them as institutions offering a broad range of learning opportunities and a developmental focus, while others can attend for specific purposes including upgrade training and short courses. The Canadian and United States community colleges, with their multiple missions, are good examples of such hybrid institutions. And those colleges that have defined themselves as comprehensive local or regional centres rather than new universities have a much better chance of developing a unique role within tertiary education, rather than remaining subordinate.

In expanding and creating tertiary institutions, all countries face a series of decisions and a series of trade-offs that are influenced both by policy makers and by the pressures of institutions themselves. These include at least the following:

• Which type of institutions to expand – universities or other types of institutions, and if the latter, of what type. This choice results partly from decisions about where enrolments are to take place. Market mechanisms are also important, and policy makers cannot dictate what the market will favour, but they can wield considerable influence through regulation and through the costs and location of alternatives.

• Whether to reinforce status hierarchies by providing different funding levels to various institutions (as most countries have done), or to moderate these hierarchies by limiting differentials in funding and quality.

• Whether to encourage narrowly focused or unitary institutions by limiting the levels and types of qualifications provided, or to stimulate multi-purpose institutions by allowing them to engage in a broader variety of entrepreneurial activities, including those specialised to localities.

• Whether to discourage the non-university institutions that provide tertiary education from establishing connections with universities, secondary schools, or labour market programmes – in which case they will remain relatively isolated institutions – or to pursue a more integrated and articulated approach to education and training.

• Whether to rely on the potentially lower costs and greater geographical accessibility of non-university institutions to provide greater access to low-income and minority students, or also to take a more active role in promoting equity by fostering a greater range of services to support students, including income and family supports to address the family-work-schooling dilemma.

• Whether to exploit the "natural" instructional advantages of institutions other than universities – smaller classes, staff dedicated to teaching rather than research, greater use of individuals from industry with up-to-date knowledge, and sometimes greater use of work-based learning – to improve the quality of teaching, or in addition to make teaching a priority through various institutional policies rather than something left to the whims of individual instructors.

• Whether to take steps to improve the economic benefits of these institutions. While countries without controls over labour markets cannot force benefits to exist, they can adopt policies to provide students with information about economic benefits, to target occupations with promising benefits, to ensure that institutions emphasise qualifications with known benefits rather than creating new qualifications of unknown value (as England has constantly done), to encourage completion and discourage dropping out, and to provide placement offices so that students can find related employment. These steps all cost additional resources, and they may constrain institutions from providing certain programmes – those with low employment and earnings levels, for example. But in an occupationally-oriented system, any institution that fails to create economic benefits is likely to find itself diminishing over time as students look elsewhere.

Forecasting is a risky business, but the future of the institutions that provide tertiary education outside of the university looks assured. The pressures to expand tertiary education continue to be strong in most developed countries, and much of this expansion will take place outside of the university, partly because of cost and locational advantages. The creation and expansion of these institutions provide students, employers, policy makers, and educators themselves with greater choices. In the next few decades the question for countries with such institutions – as well as countries contemplating reform of tertiary education and transitional countries struggling to prepare students for emerging labour markets – is how to create the right balance among different elements. This balance will involve inevitable trade-offs, and will require account to be taken of the competing needs of students, of employers, and of policy makers representing national goals. In the end, such choices can create robust institutions with their own strengths and identity, and not simply small versions of universities.

References

Achtenhagen, F. and W.N. Grubb (2001), "Vocational and Occupational Education: Pedagogical Complexity, Institutional Indifference", in V. Richardson (ed.), Handbook of Research on Teaching (4th ed.), American Educational Research Association, Washington, DC.

Bailey, B. (2002), "Further Education", in R. Aldrich (ed.), A Century of Education, Routledge Falmer, London, pp. 54-74.

Bailey, T. and I. Averianova (1998), Multiple Missions of Community Colleges: Conflicting or Complementary?, Community College Research Centre, Teachers College, Columbia University, New York, October.

Barnett, R. (2003), Beyond All Reason: Living With Ideology in the University, Open University Press, Buckingham.

Berkner, L., S. He, E.F. Cataldi and P. Knepper (2002), "Descriptive Summary of 1995-96 Beginning Postsecondary Students: Six Years Later", NCES 2003-151, National Centre for Education Statistics, U.S. Department of Education, Washington, DC, December.

Boyer, E. (1990), Scholarship Reconsidered: Priorities of the Professoriate, Carnegie Foundation for the Advancement of Teaching, Princeton.

Cereq (2003), "L'enseignement supérieur professionnalisé : un atout pour entrer dans la vie active ? ", Cereq Bref, No. 195, March, www.cereq.fr.

Dearden, L., S. McIntosh, M. Myack and A. Vignoles (2000), The Returns to Academic and Vocational Qualifications in Britain, Centre for the Economics of Education, London School of Economics and Political Science, London, November.

Dougherty, K. (1994), The Contradictory College: The Conflicting Origins, Impacts, and Futures of the Community College, State University of New York Press, Albany.

Eurydice (2000), "Two Decades of Reform in Higher Education in Europe: 1980 Onwards", www.eurydice.org.

Foucade, B. and J. Haas (2002), "L'université moins attractive ? Les transformations récentes de l'accès à l'enseignement supérieur en France et en Allemagne", Note No. 367, LIRHE, Université des Sciences Sociales, Toulouse.

Gallagher, M. (2003), "Higher Education Financing in Australia", Presentation to the Education Committee, OECD, April.

Giret, J-F., S. Moullet and G. Thomas (2002), "De l'enseignement supérieur à l'emploi : les trois premières années de vie active de la 'Génération 98'", December, *www.cereq.fr*

Gittell, M. and T. Steffy (2000), "Community Colleges Addressing Students' Needs: A Case Study of LaGuardia Community College", Howard Samuels State Management and Policy Center, City University of New York, New York, January.

Grubb, W.N. (1996), *Working in the Middle: Strengthening Education and Training for the Mid-Skilled Labor Force*, Jossey-Bass, San Francisco.

Grubb, W.N. (2002a), "Learning and Earning in the Middle, Part I: National Studies of Pre-baccalaureate Education", *Economics of Education Review*, Vol. 21, pp. 299-321.

Grubb, W.N. (2002b), "Who Am I: The Inadequacy of Career Information in the Information Age", paper prepared for the OECD Career Guidance Policy Review, *www.oecd.org/edu/careerguidance*

Grubb, W.N. (2004), "An Occupation in Harmony: The Roles of Markets and Governments in Career Information and Career Guidance", *International Journal for Educational and Vocational Guidance*.

Grubb, W.N. and Associates (1999), *Honored But Invisible: An Inside Look at Teaching Community Colleges*, Routledge, New York and London.

Grubb, W.N., N. Badway and D. Bell (2003), "Community College and the Equity Agenda: The Potential of Non-credit Education", in K. Shaw and J. Jacobs (eds.), *Community College: New Environments, New Directions. Annals of the American Academy of Political and Social Science*, Vol. 586, pp. 218-240.

Grubb, W.N. and M. Lazerson (2004), *The Education Gospel: The Economic Power of Schooling*, Harvard University Press, Cambridge.

Grubb, W.N. and J. Tuma (1991), "Who Gets Student Aid? Variations in Access to Aid", *Review of Higher Education*, Vol. 14(3), pp. 359-381.

Harkin, J. and P. Davis (1996a), "The Communications Styles of Teachers in Post-compulsory Education", *Journal of Further and Higher Education*, Vol. 20(1), pp. 25-34.

Harkin, J. and P. Davis (1996b), "The Impact of GNVQs on the Communications Styles of Teachers", *Research in Post-compulsory Education*, Vol. 1(1), pp. 97-107.

Haut Comité éducation économie emploi (HCEEE)(2003), *L'enseignement supérieur court face aux défis socio-économiques: Rapport d'activité* 2002-2003, La Documentation française.

Huisman, J. and F. Kaiser (2001), *Fixed and Fuzzy Boundaries in Higher Education: A Comparative Study of (Binary) Structures in Nine Countries*, Adviesrad voor het Wetenschaps-en Technologiebelid, The Hague, January.

Kirsch, M., Y. Beernaert and S. Norgaard (2003), *Tertiary Short Cycle Education in Europe*, EURASHE, Brussels.

Kyvik, S. and O. Skodvin (2003), "Research in the Non-university Higher Education Sector: Tensions and Dilemmas", *Higher Education*, Vol. 45, pp. 203-222.

Landau, R.T., T. Taylor and G. Wright (1996), *The Mosaic of Economic Growth*, Stanford University Press, Stanford.

Lloyd, C. and J. Payne (2002), "In Search of the High Skills Society: Some Reflections on Current Visions", SKOPE Research Paper No. 32, Centre on Skills, Knowledge, and Organisational Performance, Oxford and Warwick Universities, Summer.

Matus-Grossman, L. and S. Gooden (2002), "Opening Doors: Students' Perspectives on Juggling Work, Family, and College", MDRC, New York, July.

Mayer, K., W. Mueller and R. Pollak (2003), "Institutional Change and Inequalities of Access in German Higher Education", paper presented at the International Comparative Project on Higher Education, Prague, June 2002.

Ministère de l'Éducation nationale, de l'Enseignement supérieur et de la Recherche (2002), "Expenditure on Higher Education", *The State of Education*, No. 12, édition 2002, *www.education.gouv.fr/stateval/etat/eetat12/eetat23.htm*

National Center for Education Statistics (NCES) (2002), *The Digest of Education Statistics 2001* (NCES 2002-13), NCES, U.S. Department of Education, Washington, DC.

Norwegian Social Science Data Services (1997), *Statistics on Higher Education in Norway*, NSSDS, Bergen.

OECD (1973), *Short-Cycle Higher Education: A Search for Identity*, OECD, Paris.

OECD (1991), *Alternatives to Universities*, OECD, Paris.

OECD (1998), *Redefining Tertiary Education*, OECD, Paris.

OECD (2001), *Education Policy Analysis*, OECD, Paris.

OECD (2002a), *Education at a Glance – OECD Indicators 2002*, OECD, Paris.

OECD (2003a), *Beyond Rhetoric: Adult Learning Policies and Practices*, OECD, Paris.

OECD (2003b), *Reviews of National Policies for Education – Polytechnic Education in Finland*, OECD, Paris.

OECD (2003c), *Reviews of National Policies for Education – Tertiary Education in Switzerland*, OECD, Paris.

OECD (2003d), *Education at a Glance – OECD Indicators 2003*, OECD, Paris.

OECD (2003e), "Review of Career Guidance Policies. Country Note: Austria", OECD, Paris.

OECD (2004a), "Thematic Review of Adult Learning. Country Note: Austria", OECD, Paris.

OECD (2004b), "Thematic Review of Adult Learning. Country Note: Canada", OECD, Paris.

OECD (2004c), *Education at a Glance – OECD Indicators 2004*, OECD, Paris.

OECD (2004d), *OECD Handbook for Internationally Comparative Education Statistics – Concepts, Standards, Definitions and Classifications*, OECD, Paris.

Orr, M.T. (2002), "Community College and Secondary School Collaborations: A Case of Organisational Economics and Institutionalism", Draft paper, Community College Research Center, Teachers College, Columbia University, NY, September.

Pratt, J. (1997), *The Polytechnic Experiment 1965-1992*, Society for Research into Higher Education and Open University Press, Buckingham, United Kingdom.

Reichert, S. and C. Tauch (2003), "Trends 2003: Progress Towards the European Higher Education Area", prepared for the European University Association, European Commission, Directorate-General for Education and Culture, Brussels, July.

Rouse, C. (1995), "Democratization or Diversion: The Effect of Community Colleges on Educational Attainment", *Journal of Business and Economic Statistics*, Vol. 13(2), pp. 217-224.

Rouse, C. (1998), "Do Two-year Colleges Increase Overall Educational Attainment? Evidence from the States", *Journal of Policy Analysis and Management*, Vol. 17, pp. 595-620.

Ryan, C. (2002a), "Individual Returns to Vocational Education and Training Qualifications", National Centre for Vocational Education Research, *www.ncver.edu.au*

Ryan, C. (2002b), "What are the Longer-term Outcomes for Individuals Completing Vocational Education and Training Qualifications?", National Centre for Vocational Education Research, *www.ncver.edu.au*

Scheuer, M. and E. Schmidt (2000), "Les Fachhoschulen en Allemagne", RWI-Papiere, No. 66, Rheinisch-Westfälisches Institut für Wirtschaftsforschung.

Schuller, T., J. Preston, C. Hammond, A. Brasset-Grundy and J. Bynner (2003), *The Benefits of Learning: The Impact of Education on Health, Family Life, and Social Capital*, RoutledgeFalmer, London.

Woodlief, B., C. Thomas and G. Orozco (2003), *California's Gold: Claiming the Promise of Diversity in our Community Colleges*, California Tomorrow, Oakland, CA.

Zemsky, R., D. Shapiro, M. Ianozzi, P. Capelli and T. Bailey (1998), "The Transition from Initial Education to Working Life in the United States of America", a report to the OECD as part of a comparative study of transitions from initial education to working life in 14 member countries, Paris, OECD (*www.oecd.org/edu*).

Data for Figure 1.1

Persons aged 15 and over participating in tertiary education by type of programme, 2001 (%)

	Tertiary-type B	Tertiary-type A	Advanced research programmes	Total tertiary
Switzerland	0.6	2.0	0.2	2.7
Germany[1]	0.5	2.5	m	3.0
Czech Republic	0.3	2.5	0.2	3.0
Mexico	0.1	3.0	0.0	3.1
Slovak Republic	0.1	3.0	0.2	3.3
Turkey	0.8	2.5	0.0	3.4
Italy	0.1	3.5	0.0	3.7
Japan	0.9	2.7	0.1	3.7
Netherlands	0.1	3.8	0.1	3.9
Hungary	0.1	3.7	0.1	3.9
Austria	0.4	3.2	0.4	3.9
France	1.0	3.0	0.2	4.2
Belgium	2.2	2.0	0.1	4.2
United Kingdom	1.3	2.8	0.2	4.3
Denmark	0.4	3.9	0.1	4.4
Portugal	0.1	4.2	0.1	4.5
Iceland	0.4	4.3	0.0	4.7
Canada	1.2	3.5	0.1	4.8
Sweden	0.2	4.5	0.3	4.9
Norway	0.4	4.8	0.1	5.3
Greece	1.7	3.5	0.1	5.3
Spain	0.6	4.6	0.2	5.4
Ireland	2.1	3.4	0.1	5.5
Australia	1.2	4.2	0.2	5.6
Poland	0.1	5.5	0.1	5.7
New Zealand	1.5	4.3	0.1	6.0
United States	1.4	4.8	0.1	6.3
Finland	0.2	5.9	0.5	6.6
Korea	3.4	4.8	0.1	8.4

1. Advanced research programmes are missing.
Source: OECD.

Data for Figure 1.2

Total enrolments in selected non-university tertiary institutions, by ISCED level,[1] 2001[2] (%)

	ISCED levels						
	2	3	4	5B	5A	6	Total
Australia (TAFE colleges)	23	51	12	14	0	0	100
Austria (upper secondary vocational schools)	0	68	28	4	0	0	100
Japan (colleges of technology)	0	60	0	40	0	0	100
Austria (*Akademien*)	0	0	0	100	0	0	100
France (IUTs)	0	0	0	100	0	0	100
New Zealand (polytechnics)	0	48	20	18	15	0	100
Canada (community colleges)	0	0	32	48	20	0	100
Ireland (institutes of technology)	0	0	11	64	26	<1	100
Norway (university colleges)	0	0	1	6	93	<1	100
Netherlands (*Hogescholen*)	0	0	0	2	98	0	100
Austria (FHS)	0	0	0	0	100	0	100
Finland (polytechnics)	0	0	0	0	100	0	100
Germany (FHS)	0	0	0	0	100	0	100

Note: Entries are arranged in order of the percentages of total enrolments at ISCED 5A and 6.
1. ISCED levels 4-6 are defined in Box 1.1. ISCED level 2 refers to lower secondary education, and ISCED level 3 to upper secondary education.
2. Or nearest year.
Source: OECD.

Data for Figure 1.3

Relative earnings[1] by level of educational attainment, 25-to-64-year-olds, 2002[2]

	Year	Tertiary-types 5A and 6	Tertiary-type 5B
Spain	2001	141	95
Australia	2001	148	106
Korea	1998	147	106
Sweden	2001	148	110
Denmark	2001	127	114
Belgium	2002	152	114
Canada	2001	177	115
United States	2002	195	118
Germany	2002	161	120
Finland	2001	181	121
Ireland	2000	163	124
France	2002	167	125
OECD average	-	164	126
United Kingdom	2001	174	128
Netherlands	1997	144	139
Portugal	1999	192	141
Switzerland	2003	168	141
Czech Republic	1999	180	151
Norway	2002	135	155
Hungary	2001	210	164

1. Upper secondary education = 100.
2. Or nearest year.
Source: OECD (2004c).

Chapter 2

GETTING RETURNS FROM INVESTING IN EDUCATIONAL ICT

▼

SUMMARY

All OECD countries have invested heavily in ICT in schools. The equipment is being deployed for a range of purposes including improving school information systems and teaching ICT skills. But is it also being used to improve teaching and learning?

Country differences in the quantity of hardware and software remain important. Just as important is the amount that students use computers. Many students still do not use computers very much at school. Students more often use computers to send emails and access the Internet than to use educational software. One of the most important contributions to learning can be in helping low achieving students become more confident.

The biggest barriers preventing computers from transforming learning concern the capacity of teachers to integrate them into their practices, limited by organisational or time constraints or their own knowledge. Change will only be possible when improvements in the capacity to use computers are combined effectively with other forms of educational innovation.

1. INTRODUCTION

Successive waves of technology – film projectors, video cassette recorders, computers – have been enthusiastically adopted within education: the new technologies have been seen as a key to educational reform and improvement. Enthusiasm for the potential of information and communications technology (ICT) to improve the quality of teaching and learning has occurred in two phases. In the 1980s, computer aided instruction appeared to provide an opportunity to standardise teaching, reduce variation in student performance arising from varying teacher quality, and reduce teaching costs. Since the mid-1990s the rapidly falling cost of personal computers, the capacity to integrate personal computers with other forms of information technology, the advent of the Internet, and the ease with which these technologies can be networked, have revived enthusiasm for the use of ICT within education. For some, these new forms of ICT are an opportunity to tailor teaching and learning strategies more closely to individual student needs and learning styles, raising performance in key educational skills. For others, the new technologies provide a key to unlocking the dream of lifelong learning: making it possible for learning to be separated from the confines of time and space represented by the timetable and the classroom; giving learners more control over their learning through making access to important information independent of the teacher; making co-operative learning possible; bringing a wider range of learning providers into the circle; allowing key learning skills such as information search and problem solving to develop; making learning more student-centred.

Box 2.1 **National policies for ICT in education: Korea and New Zealand**

Korea's national plan for ICT in education focused, in its initial 1996-2001 stage, upon putting ICT infrastructure in place. By the completion of the first stage all schools were connected to the Internet, and all classrooms had at least one PC. There were ten students per computer in elementary schools, seven in middle schools, and six in high schools. All teachers had a PC/notebook. The second stage of the plan, which covers the 2001-2005 period, concentrates upon the purposes of ICT and the ways in which ICT is used. The plan is firmly centred around the goals of ensuring that the education system can assist Korea to become a knowledge-based society. The goals of the national strategy include: ensuring that the entire nation can develop ICT skills for a knowledge-based society; creating an information culture in Korea with equal access to information; and improving the effectiveness of the ways in which ICT is used in education. Within primary and secondary education the steps to be adopted include: revamping the curriculum to increase computer literacy and computer use so that ICT can enhance the country's competitiveness; ensuring that ICT is integrated into the curriculum of all subjects; using ICT to promote co-operative learning and information search and sharing; the development of multimedia educational materials and software; and staff development (so that one third of teachers take ICT training each year) encompassing both teachers' ICT skills and training in the use of ICT for teaching. The national strategy also encompasses ICT in tertiary education, including the establishment of a cyber university; the adoption of ICT within adult learning; and the increasing use of ICT to make educational administration more effective by, for example, improving student and parent access to student information.

New Zealand's 2002-04 strategy for ICT in schools focuses upon students, teachers, school principals, school communities, the curriculum, and ICT infrastructure. Its goals include using ICT to: develop higher-order thinking and information skills; extend teachers'

...

and school principals' ICT capacities through both inter-school co-operation and on line activities; build partnerships in ICT use between schools and their communities; and develop quality online learning resources. All schools were to be provided with high-speed Internet access by the end of 2004. The strategy has included providing all school principals with laptops, giving all permanent full-time secondary teachers the opportunity to lease a laptop, and a "Computers in Homes" initiative targeted at students from low income and disadvantaged schools.

Sources: Woo and Pang (2002) and Ministry of Education and Human Resource Development and Korea Education and Research Information Service (2002). See also *www.moe.go.kr* and *www.keris.or.kr*; Ministry of Education, New Zealand (2002) and *www.minedu.govt.nz*

Box 2.1 provides two examples of the ways in which countries have been developing policies for the use of ICT in education. These show how ICT is coming closer to the centre of educational policy making. Yet at the same time there have been dissenting voices. Cuban (2001) for example argues that the new technologies have been "oversold and underused". Zemsky and Massy (2004) argue that use of the Internet and other technologies as learning platforms have not delivered the results industry experts anticipated. Elsewhere the OECD has described use of ICT in schools as "... disappointing, particularly when compared with the diffusion of ICTs in other parts of society" (OECD, 2004c, p. 235). This chapter draws upon OECD evidence to describe patterns of investment in ICT, largely within secondary schools,[1] and to assess whether the educational returns that have been gained from ICT have been commensurate with the level of investment. It explores barriers that are preventing schools from realising their ICT-related goals, and concludes by suggesting what needs to be done if countries are to gain improved educational benefits from their investments in educational ICT.

2. INVESTMENTS IN EDUCATIONAL ICT

All OECD countries have invested heavily in ICT within their education systems over the last decade. The absolute scale of this investment is not easy to quantify. A quite rough estimate for the late 1990s by the OECD's Centre for Educational Research and Innovation (CERI) put the annual investment, across all OECD countries, at around USD 16 billion (OECD, 1999).

While it is difficult to accurately estimate the level of investment in educational ICT across OECD countries, a useful proxy indicator of relative levels of investment is the number of students per computer: the lower this number, the higher the investment. Data gathered for PISA, the OECD's Programme for International Student Assessment, provide such an indicator for 15-year-old school students in 2003. Figure 2.1 shows that in 2003, the number of 15-year-old students per computer ranged from a low of 3 to a high of 25. These figures suggest that investment in ICT has been around four to five times or more higher in countries such as Australia, Hungary, Korea, New Zealand, the United Kingdom and the United States than in countries such as Poland, the Slovak Republic and Turkey.[2] Neither overall national wealth nor the relative priority that countries place upon educational expenditure can explain most of the variation between countries in their levels of investment in educational ICT (Box 2.2).

---

1. Comparable data that can shed light upon patterns of investment in ICT in other sectors of education such as primary schooling and tertiary education are not available.

2. Computers are, of course, only one form of investment in educational ICT. Additional investments are made in software, peripheral devices such as printers and scanners, Internet connections, local networks, teacher training, maintenance and support staff.

| Figure 2.1 | Mean number of 15-year-old students per computer, 2003 |

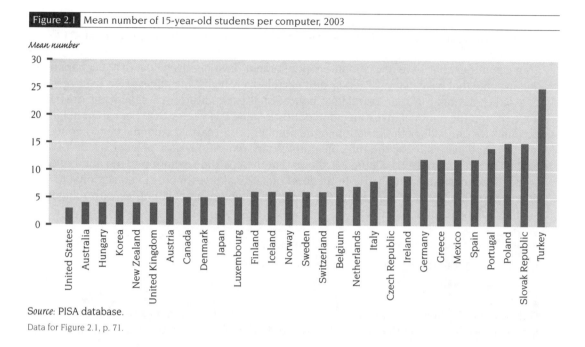

Source: PISA database.

Data for Figure 2.1, p. 71.

It is also clear that ICT investments in education have grown at a rapid rate in recent years. This has been stimulated by growth in computing power for a fixed unit of investment, by the increasing accessibility of the Internet, and by the new educational possibilities afforded by both. There are now signs of convergence between countries on at least some indicators of students' access to ICT. Two sets of OECD data indicate the scale of this growth. The first is the OECD's International Survey of Upper Secondary Schools (ISUSS) (OECD, 2004a), which shows very rapid development in the availability of ICT in schools between the mid-1990s and 2001. In that survey school principals were asked to estimate the year in which three ICT elements were introduced to their school: standard software applications such as word processing and spreadsheets; access to the Internet; and e-mail. Across the 11 countries for which comparable data were available, the proportion of students attending schools with access to the Internet grew from 24% to 97% between 1995 and 2001 (Figure 2.3), so earlier inequalities in access have greatly reduced. In the same period the percentage of students attending schools where teachers and students used e-mail grew from 13% to 89% and the proportion attending schools where standard software packages were used grew from 80% to 98% (OECD, 2004a). Data from the United States show that over a similar period (1994-2000) the proportion of public schools with access to the Internet grew from 35% to 98%. Even more strikingly, the proportion of public schools' individual classrooms with Internet access grew from only 3% to 77% (National Center for Education Statistics, 2001).

The very rapid speed with which ICT has been penetrating schools in OECD countries in more recent years is illustrated by a comparison between the number of 15-year-old students per computer revealed by the 2000 and 2003 PISA surveys: investment levels in most countries appear to have at least doubled in only a three-year period. In countries such as Greece, Mexico and Portugal, where very few computers were available for 15-year-old students in 2000, investments grew by a factor of five or more. For example in Mexico the number of students per computer fell from 81 to 12 over the period, and in Greece it fell from 58 to 12. Even in countries where the number of students per computer was already low in 2000, investments seem to have close to doubled in a very short period. In the United States the number of students per computer halved: from six to three. In Denmark it fell from ten to five (Table 2.1).

Box 2.2 **How much does national income determine investments in educational ICT?**

Some countries that have few computers per student have relatively low GDP per capita, and in some that have many, GDP per capita is relatively high. This might seem to suggest that either national income or relative educational expenditure is a significant driving force behind the national investments in educational ICT. However GDP per capita in fact accounts for only 42% of the variation in the number of 15-year-old students per computer in 2003, and national expenditure on non-tertiary education as a percentage of GDP explains even less: only 2%. Figure 2.2 shows that there is wide variation in the number of students per computer, and hence in the level of national investments in educational ICT, at any given level of GDP per capita. For example among pairs of countries with roughly similar GDP per capita:

- Turkey had twice as many students per computer as Mexico.
- Spain had about three times as many as New Zealand.
- Germany had about three times as many as Australia.

Hungary and Korea are other countries in which the level of investment in educational ICT for 15-year-olds is higher than would be expected on the basis of national wealth alone.

| Figure 2.2 | Students per computer and GDP per capita, 2003 |

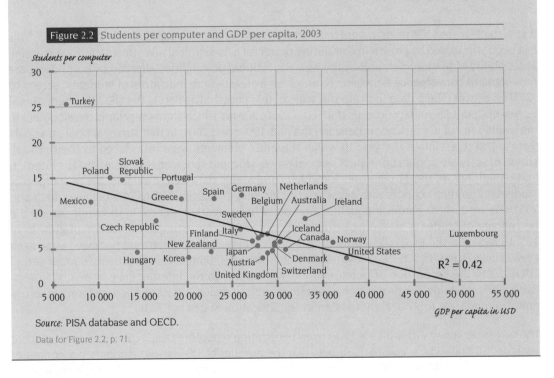

Source: PISA database and OECD.

Data for Figure 2.2, p. 71.

During the rapid expansion in investments in educational ICT that started in the mid-1990s, policy efforts in OECD countries, particularly within schools, concentrated upon equipping educational institutions with hardware and software, and, to a lesser extent, upon trying to ensure that teachers were able to use the new technologies. As the level of investment has grown, and as the technology has become more pervasive, attention is increasingly turning to how ICT can be integrated into the curriculum, and into the teaching and learning process in order to produce better learning outcomes.

Table 2.1 Mean number of students per computer, 2000 and 2003		
	2000	2003
United States	6	3
Australia	6	4
New Zealand	7	4
Norway	7	6
United Kingdom	8	4
Korea	10	4
Austria	10	5
Denmark	10	5
Luxembourg	10	5
Finland	10	6
Iceland	11	6
Hungary	12	4
Switzerland	12	6
Sweden	12	6
Japan	14	5
Belgium	15	7
Italy	16	8
Ireland	16	9
Spain	24	12
Germany	24	12
Czech Republic	26	9
Poland	40	15
Greece	58	12
Portugal	74	14
Mexico	81	12

Source: PISA database.

Figure 2.3 Percentage of upper secondary students attending schools with access to the Internet, 1995 and 2001

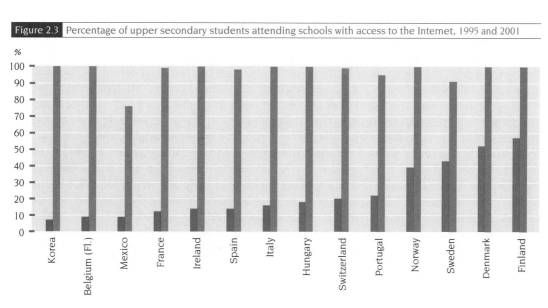

Source: OECD (2004a, Table 3.7).

Data for Figure 2.3, p. 72.

3. ASSESSING THE EDUCATIONAL IMPACT OF ICT

3.1. Why have countries invested in educational ICT?

There have been several reasons for countries equipping schools, tertiary education and adult learning institutions with ICT:

- One reason, although probably not the most important, has been a belief that ICT can help to reduce the cost of education: making some of its ancillary processes (enrolling students, keeping track of lending books from libraries, managing large assessment systems, personnel records and the like) more efficient; or reducing the teaching costs that are at the heart of education.

- A second, and more important reason, has been to ensure that nations are not left behind in a world in which information-based technology is an important source of economic growth and enterprise productivity (OECD, 2003a; OECD, 2004b), and in which ICT is strongly linked to the upskilling of the labour force (Green, Felstead and Gallie, 2000). Closely related to this is parents' and students' concern that the education system should equip young people with the skills that are important for individual success in the labour market (OECD, 2004c).

- A third reason is the belief that ICT is now an essential tool for everyone living in knowledge-based societies so that all citizens – young people and adults – need to acquire a minimum level of ICT competence. This has made ICT important in school education (OECD, 2004c) as well as resulting in it becoming a significant issue in adult education in many OECD countries (Selwyn, 2003).

- A fourth reason, a main focus of this chapter, has been the belief that ICT offers a powerful tool to improve the outcomes of education: to improve the quality of teaching and to improve the quality of students' learning (OECD, 2001).

- A fifth reason has been to improve management and accountability processes within education: for example by improving the information available to classroom teachers on student performance, and the information that is available to educational managers on outcomes at the school and system level.

The multiplicity of policy goals, which can be seen in the examples given in Box 2.1, complicates the task of evaluating the impact of such investments. Each can lead to different decisions about appropriate hardware, software, operating systems, curriculum content, student access, teacher training strategies and the like. For example, the need to create a cadre of highly-skilled ICT specialists could result in the concentration of equipment in computer laboratories with limited student access. A need to ensure that all citizens are computer literate would provide broad access to all students and adults, with a focus upon the software and operating systems commonly found in everyday life and in the commercial world. A focus upon improving teaching and learning, on the other hand, would require wide student access from an early age, might focus ICT resources in the compulsory years of schooling where the foundations of learning skills are laid, and would put resources into the development and use of specialised educational software, and into teacher training strategies that focus upon the improvement of pedagogical skills with ICT, not just upon using common applications packages. Within any one country all of these approaches may be occurring at once.

A further complication, when trying to assess the educational impact of ICT, is that countries can have different expectations about the ways in which ICT might be able to improve educational outcomes. The educational goals of one might not reflect those of another. Two broad positions on the benefits that should be expected from investing in educational ICT can be observed. On the one hand there is a view, perhaps illustrated most clearly in the case of the United States (see for example Archbald, 2001), that ICT can be judged by the extent to which it is able to improve student performance on standardised tests. Another view, perhaps illustrated best in some of the Nordic countries, is that ICT is an ideal tool for the achievement of lifelong learning: raising the motivation to learn (by giving learners more control over the content, timing and mode of their learning); and developing key learning skills such as co-operative learning, problem solving, information acquisition and analysis, and autonomous learning. See for example Castells and Himanen (2002); Delegation for ICT in Schools (2002); Ministry of Education, Denmark (1998).

This chapter does not try to reconcile these several perspectives. Rather it looks at evidence on the extent to which computers are used in schools and the purposes for which they are being used, regardless of such different rationales. It goes on to look at barriers to access and use.

3.2. The extent of computer use

In some OECD countries many students are likely to have considerable difficulty in gaining access to computers. For example in Germany, Greece, Mexico, Poland, Portugal, the Slovak Republic, Spain and Turkey there are 12 or more 15-year-old students for each computer (Figure 2.1). In such countries, it is likely that only some students can gain enough access for this to have an educational impact. On the other hand in countries such as Australia, Hungary, Korea, New Zealand, the United Kingdom and the United States the number of students per computer (three to four) is small enough. This means that more students are likely to get access to computers, and to use them at school.

Having computers in a school is one thing. Using them is another. Drawing on data from the 2003 PISA survey, Table 2.2 shows that quite different patterns of computer use can exist in countries with the same ratio of students per computer. Even in countries with highest levels of investment in ICT in schools, computers do not seem to be used most of the time. For example Hungary and Korea had the same number of students per computer in 2003 (four). However in Korea 42% of 15-year-old students used a computer at school less than once a month or never, compared to only 9% in Hungary. Denmark and Japan both had five 15-year-old students per computer. However in Denmark 68% of 15-year-olds use a computer almost every day or a few times a week, but in Japan only 26% use it this often at school. Germany and Mexico each had one computer for every 12 15-year-old students. Yet in Germany only 23% of 15-year-olds used a computer almost every day or a few times each week, compared to 54% in Mexico.

Table 2.2 also shows that in only a handful of countries do computers appear to have become an every day piece of equipment in the school. Denmark, Hungary and the United Kingdom are the only countries in which two thirds or more of 15-year-olds use a computer at school either almost every day or a few times each week.

These patterns point to significant under-utilisation of investment in the ICT that is available in schools in some OECD countries. Another explanation could be that in some countries the use of computers in schools is heavily concentrated among a relatively small group of students. Whichever is the case, the outcome would be a less than optimal impact of ICT on most students' learning.

The data in Table 2.2 have been used to construct an index of the average frequency with which 15-year-old students use computers at school. The values of this index can be compared to an identical index constructed from the same question in the PISA 2000 ICT questionnaire. The index for 2003 shows that 15-year-old students use computers at school most frequently in Australia,

Denmark, Hungary and the United Kingdom. All were countries that were leaders in the use of computers by 15-year-olds in 2000 (Figure 2.4). The countries in which computers were used least frequently by 15-year-old students in 2003 were Germany, Ireland, Japan and Korea. Although the sample of countries for which this index can be constructed was smaller in 2000 than in 2003, Germany and Ireland were also countries in which 15-year-old students had relatively little contact with computers at school in 2000.

In nearly all countries for which values of the index can be calculated in 2000 and 2003, Figure 2.4 shows that the average frequency of use rose in three years. In the Czech Republic and Mexico average use rose by 34% and 65% respectively over the period, and in Germany it rose by 27%. However in Ireland and Finland average use fell, even if only slightly, over the period, and in Belgium there was no change.

Table 2.2 Students per computer and frequency of use of computers at school, 2003

		15-year-olds using computers at school (%):				
	15-year-old students per computer	Almost every day	A few times each week	Between once a week and once a month	Less than once a month	Never
United States	3	20	23	28	21	8
Australia	4	15	44	27	11	3
Hungary	4	6	74	10	4	5
Korea	4	4	25	29	14	28
New Zealand	4	21	22	26	23	8
United Kingdom	4	23	48	15	10	5
Austria	5	11	42	31	9	7
Canada	5	15	26	31	21	8
Denmark	5	23	45	25	6	1
Japan	5	2	24	33	16	25
Finland	6	4	32	41	18	5
Iceland	6	5	36	40	13	6
Sweden	6	15	33	30	15	6
Switzerland	6	3	27	36	21	13
Belgium	7	2	25	35	19	20
Italy	8	4	47	20	11	18
Czech Republic	9	5	36	44	7	8
Ireland	9	2	22	27	16	32
Germany	12	1	22	28	27	21
Greece	12	4	41	27	9	19
Mexico	12	8	46	16	10	20
Portugal	14	5	29	25	26	15
Poland	15	2	42	34	10	12
Slovak Republic	15	4	38	30	7	21
Turkey	25	7	39	8	6	40

Source: PISA database.

Figure 2.4 Average frequency with which 15-year-old students used computers at school, 2000 and 2003

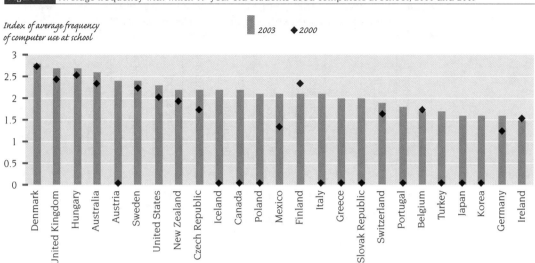

Note: A value of 0.0 on the index corresponds to "Never"; a value of 1 to "Less than once a month"; a value of 2 to "Between once a week and once a month"; a value of 3 to "A few times each week" and a value of 4 to "Almost every day".

Source: PISA database.

Data for Figure 2.4, p. 72.

3.3. What are the computers used for?

Two OECD school surveys shed light upon the ways in which young people are using computers. The ICT questionnaire in PISA 2003 contained twelve questions asking students how often they used computers for specific purposes. Whilst it did not distinguish between use at school and use in other locations such as the home, the responses, which are summarised in Table 2.3, shed interesting light on the educational benefits that might result from the use of ICT by 15-year-olds.

Across the OECD as a whole, 15-year-olds most commonly report that they use computers frequently for electronic communication (e-mail or chat rooms), to surf the web (which might, of course, be for school-related purposes), and to play games, followed by downloading music and word processing. Educational software is the least common type of use, followed by programming and spreadsheets. Of the twelve items included in the questionnaire, using computers to learn school material was ranked eighth. In all of the 25 countries educational software was the least common type of frequent use for computers. Across the OECD as a whole, an average of 49% of 15-year-olds reported that they never use educational software, and 28% that they never use computers for learning school material. Only in Mexico, Poland and Turkey did as many as a quarter of 15-year-olds say that they use educational software almost every day or a few times a week. And only in Denmark and Portugal did half or more of all 15-year-olds report that they used computers to learn school material almost every day or a few times a week. The difference between the intensity with which 15-year-olds use computers for purposes such as surfing the web and playing games on the one hand, and the frequency with which they use them for obviously school-related purposes on the other, is quite striking. For example in Sweden, 75% of 15-year-olds use computers fairly frequently for electronic communication. Yet only 5% regularly use educational software, and only 23% regularly use computers to help them with school work.[3]

---

3. In Japan only 11% of 15-year-olds reported that they used computers frequently for anything. This raises the intriguing possibility that a focus upon the use of computers is too narrow, and that increasing attention should be paid to the ways in which young people use other electronic media such as mobile phones.

| Table 2.3 | 15-year-olds reporting that computers are used either almost every day or a few times a week for twelve specific purposes, 2003 (%) |

	Electronic communication	Internet search	Games	Internet music downloads	Word processing	Internet software downloads	Internet collaboration	Learning school material	Drawing, painting, graphics	Programming	Spreadsheets	Educational software
Australia	69	74	50	58	70	47	43	32	32	25	22	10
Austria	58	62	43	50	60	38	26	31	28	23	25	9
Belgium	71	60	50	58	49	44	33	24	19	23	17	7
Canada	83	75	59	77	62	58	49	29	35	29	17	9
Czech Republic	48	54	53	33	46	27	30	26	28	19	22	15
Denmark	63	68	58	43	65	38	34	51	22	20	18	15
Finland	59	40	53	38	27	30	13	18	18	11	6	3
Germany	54	53	52	48	49	37	21	27	24	23	19	11
Greece	36	45	61	50	45	46	26	23	45	28	27	22
Hungary	48	42	61	33	53	24	33	31	30	17	32	10
Iceland	71	73	53	33	44	43	25	38	23	22	14	11
Ireland	34	38	47	58	34	24	17	16	26	13	15	9
Italy	41	54	57	47	59	44	25	44	41	31	31	20
Japan	22	26	19	12	17	9	7	5	9	3	8	1
Korea	73	59	57	79	32	47	49	19	15	8	7	6
Mexico	47	50	45	46	38	36	40	45	48	32	32	25
New Zealand	69	65	56	58	54	47	39	30	33	25	22	12
Poland	45	44	56	40	47	32	38	26	40	28	32	25
Portugal	53	58	60	50	53	41	44	57	29	34	28	15
Slovak Republic	29	36	57	23	44	19	26	32	33	20	23	18
Sweden	75	62	57	62	47	44	28	23	25	18	8	5
Switzerland	58	57	43	47	45	37	26	20	22	21	19	8
Turkey	43	38	56	47	43	40	29	32	45	37	32	26
United Kingdom	69	65	58	58	66	49	41	34	36	27	31	19
United States	71	74	62	64	62	52	42	36	41	33	22	18
Average	56	55	53	49	48	38	31	30	30	23	21	13

Source: PISA database.

Indeed between the 2000 and 2003 PISA surveys there appears to have been a decline in some of the more explicitly educational use of computers by 15-year-olds. For those countries for which comparable data are available for both surveys, Table 2.4 shows the percentage of 15-year-olds who in each survey reported that they either used computers to learn school material or used educational software either almost every day or several times a week. For each of these uses the average across the 15 countries declined in the period. In all 15 countries the reported use of educational software fell, with the average decline being around 50%. In the case of using computers to learn school material the average decline was smaller, but in some countries such as Ireland and the United Kingdom it was quite marked.

Table 2.4 15-year-old students reporting that they frequently[1] use computers to learn school material or that they frequently use educational software, 2000 and 2003 (%)

	School material, 2000	School material, 2003	Educational software, 2000	Educational software, 2003
Australia	43	32	23	10
Belgium	21	24	18	7
Canada	32	29	18	9
Czech Republic	18	26	19	15
Denmark	54	51	11	15
Finland	24	18	8	3
Germany	33	27	23	11
Hungary	26	31	19	10
Ireland	25	16	26	9
Mexico	54	45	38	25
New Zealand	38	30	26	12
Sweden	39	23	12	5
Switzerland	21	20	13	8
United Kingdom	57	34	34	19
United States	47	36	28	18
Average	35	29	21	12

1. Frequently indicates either almost every day or a few times each week.
Source: PISA database.

A cautious conclusion about the real extent to which ICT is being used in schools to improve teaching and learning emerges from data gathered in the OECD's International Survey of Upper Secondary Schools. In that survey, school principals were asked the extent to which students used computers for six different purposes, and in this instance the questions focused strongly on pedagogical processes (see Table 2.5). Getting information from the Internet was the most commonly reported use, with around two thirds of upper secondary students across all OECD countries being reported to do this a lot. In Sweden half or more, and in Norway nearly half, of all upper secondary students are reported to use computers frequently to develop independent learning skills or to supplement the teacher. In Denmark around 40% of upper secondary students are reported to use computers a lot to develop independent learning skills and to combine parts of subjects. However in other countries, fewer students are reported to use ICT frequently for this purpose – in Ireland and Spain, fewer than one student in six.[4]

---

4. A similar conclusion emerges from the IEA international TIMSS reports which show that even in countries with high classroom availability, the use of computers in over half of all lessons is extremely rare at 4th and 8th grades in maths and science (*http://isc.bc.edu/timss2003i/intl_reports.html*).

Table 2.5 **Percentage of upper secondary students attending schools where principals report that computers are used a lot for various educational purposes, 2001**

	Obtaining information from the Internet	Developing skills of independent learning	Providing additional instruction and practice opportunities	Allowing students to learn/work at their own pace	Combining parts of school subjects	Learning by simulation
Belgium (Fl.)	64	18	15	13	6	7
Denmark	93	39	23	32	44	22
Finland	75	22	13	9	7	4
France	65	35	6	13	21	16
Hungary	73	18	7	17	21	27
Ireland	43	15	24	6	3	4
Italy	53	37	29	17	37	28
Korea	80	37	11	31	17	17
Mexico	37	37	26	41	29	11
Norway	95	42	52	20	20	14
Portugal	59	30	18	21	13	18
Spain	37	16	10	11	8	13
Sweden	91	58	49	25	20	13
Switzerland	72	33	12	13	18	12
Average	67	31	21	19	19	15

Source: OECD (2004a, Table 3.14a).

The OECD's work on adult learning (OECD, 2003b; Pont and Sweet, 2003) highlights many innovative uses of ICT to improve teaching and learning within the corporate world and in post-secondary education. However outside of these settings, and in particular within community settings and in those locations where the least qualified adults undertake courses of study, it points to a relatively limited use of ICT to improve the quality of teaching and learning. Selwyn (2003) highlights evidence from the United Kingdom indicating that the most common purpose of ICT courses offered within adult education settings is to develop basic ICT literacy. A number of countries however have launched projects to combine the teaching of ICT skills with the use of ICT as a tool to deliver course content. The *Aulas Mentor* in Spain, the *Plazas Communitarias* in Mexico and the Transformer Bus in the United States (OECD, 2003b) are programmes that have managed to reach especially disadvantaged adults to use ICT for learning. In the United Kingdom Learndirect provides an information technology platform for learning in easily accessible places.

The evidence reviewed above suggests that we cannot assume that large investments in ICT have everywhere had a large positive impact on learning outcomes. Nevertheless, for some schools and students the impact of being well supplied with ICT, and of the available equipment being used effectively, might bring benefits. Case studies can help to shed some light on this, and these are drawn upon in Section 6 below. First, however, the following section considers more specifically evidence about whether the use of ICT improves learning.

4. CAN ICT IMPROVE LEARNING?

Existing experimental studies provide little guidance overall on the impact of contemporary forms of ICT upon learning outcomes, and even less on their impact upon the motivation to learn or the development of key learning skills. This is for two reasons: it is hard for such evidence to pick up the wider learning outcomes that ICT might be expected to improve; and it is hard for research to keep up-to-date with the rapidly evolving potential of technology.

First, much of the existing research is fairly narrowly focused upon a limited range of learning outcomes that are easily measurable, such as scores on standard tests, and upon activities and school subjects such as mathematics in which large numbers of students participate so that sample sizes can be maximised. This ignores the enormously diverse ways in which modern ICT is currently being used within education in all OECD countries. In schools it is now common to see ICT being used by students to write essays, find information for projects and assignments, compose music, share ideas with students in other schools, conduct simulations, build databases, create works of art and do detailed architectural drawings. Frequently only small numbers may be doing any one of these at any one time, and the outcomes of what they are doing may be difficult to measure.

The second limitation of much of the existing experimental evidence is that it is dated. Large studies take a long while to conduct, to analyse and to report, and as a result are often useful largely as a guide to yesterday's technologies and yesterday's pedagogy. For example a recent large scale and widely reported study of the impact of ICT upon mathematics and language scores (Angrist and Lavy, 2002) was carried out between 1994 and 1996, before the Internet became a common tool or educational ICT was widely networked, and studied computer aided instruction on stand-alone PCs. A third limitation is that many studies are not strong methodologically, with poor designs and inappropriate analyses.

Within these constraints, syntheses of the existing research such as Kulik (2003) and Torgerson and Zhu (2003) provide some qualified support for proponents of the use of ICT to improve learning. The outcomes for reading skills are unclear but point to inadequate implementation strategies. However evaluations do support the capacity of word processors, or simply access to computers and to the Internet, to develop writing skills. They also provide some support for the proposition that ICT can at times improve outcomes in mathematics and the natural sciences, although individual effects are often weak and findings are inconsistent. Similarly a recent large United Kingdom study (Impact2) has shown statistically significant relationships between use of ICT and attainment at several stages of education (BECTA, 2002). As well as raising performance on standardised tests, an important potential benefit of the use of ICT is to raise performance indirectly by strengthening the motivation to learn and developing learning skills. As described below, evidence suggests that this can be especially valuable for low achievers.

4.1. ICT and low achieving students

Whether countries see ICT as a tool to improve standard test scores or to improve the motivation to learn and learning skills, the greatest overall gains will result from improving outcomes for the lowest achievers: their potential gains are greater than those whose achievement levels are already high. PISA 2000 data can help to shed light on whether, and in what ways, ICT might help to improve learning outcomes among low achievers, and on some of the barriers to improvement. In addition to gathering data on student achievement in literacy, mathematics and science, the first round of PISA data collection in 2000 included a special student computer familiarity questionnaire. Questions about ICT availability and use were also included in the main questionnaire completed by all students and in the school questionnaire completed by school principals.[5] Using PISA data, Sweet and Meates (2004) provide an initial report on the relationship between 15-year-olds' literacy achievement levels and access to and patterns of use of ICT. This analysis provides some encouraging messages, but also many challenges for schools in ensuring that the weakest students can benefit from using ICT.

---

5. The IT questionnaire, the student questionnaire, and the school questionnaire can be found at *www.pisa.oecd.org*

One generally encouraging message to emerge from analysis of PISA data is that within many OECD countries the number of students per computer in the schools in which the weakest students[6] are located is generally no lower than the number of students per computer in other schools. And there are some countries – Denmark, Germany, Italy, Japan, Korea, the Netherlands and Portugal – in which the schools where the lowest achievers are concentrated are the ones that have the greatest number of computers. These are important findings. There are some exceptions however. In the Czech Republic, France, Mexico and Poland, low achieving students tend to be located in schools with the highest number of students per computer.[7] In Mexico, for example, the number of students per computer is around six times as high in the schools where the weakest students are found as it is in the schools containing the most able students (129 compared to 21). And in France the number of students per computer is around 50% greater in schools where the lowest achievers are located than in the schools where the highest achievers are located (15 compared to 10).

Another encouraging message is that in all OECD countries, low achieving 15-year-olds seem to be just as interested in using computers as other students. No statistically significant differences emerge on a scale of interest in ICT between the scores of the lowest literacy achievers and other students.

Figure 2.5 Mean number of computers in the homes of the lowest and highest achievers, 2000

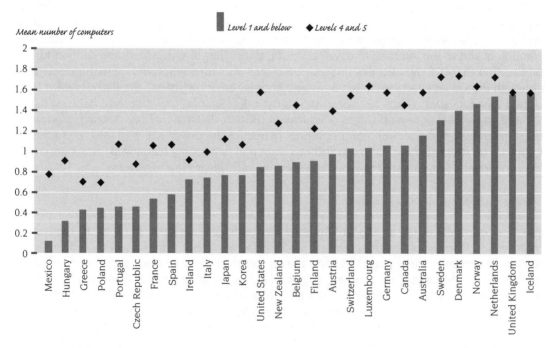

Source: PISA database.

Data for Figure 2.5, p. 73.

6. Defined as those scoring at Level 1 or below on the PISA combined reading literacy scale. The study defined high achievers as those scoring at Levels 4 and 5 on the combined reading literacy scale.

7. In the case of France the explanation is likely to be that weaker 15-year-old students are more likely to be in a *collège* and the better students in a *lycée*.

A further finding of importance to schools is that in nearly all OECD countries, low achievers' access to ICT is both greater, and more equitable, in the school than it is in the home. There is an extremely strong and significant trend for low achievers to report less access to ICT in the home than do high achievers. Figure 2.5 compares the number of computers in the homes of the lowest achievers with the number in the homes of the highest achievers. In the United States, as an example, the average number of computers in the homes of those scoring at Level 1 or below on the PISA combined reading literacy scale is 0.8, compared to 1.6 in the homes of those scoring at Levels 4 and 5: half as many. In Hungary, there is an average of 0.3 computers in the homes of the lowest achievers, compared to 0.9 in the homes of the highest achievers: one third as many. Similar trends emerge when access to the Internet and the use of educational software in the home are analysed. So schools, in most OECD countries, cannot assume that if low achievers do not get access to ICT in school the home will compensate. The reverse is true. There is a very strong digital divide in the home as a function of literacy level, and this is much less evident in the school. Schools and school systems have, as a result, an important role to play in helping to ensure that low achievers have access to ICT, either within normal school hours or through special programmes outside of them.

The analysis presents schools with a number of other challenges. For example when those schools in which computers are scarce are analysed, it is generally more common for low achievers to report that they have little access to computers than it is for high achievers. And so within-school practices are just as important in ensuring access to ICT as is the general availability of computers across schools.

Another challenge is to raise the motivation and confidence of low achievers in using ICT. While in all countries low achieving 15-year-olds are just as interested in computers as are other students, in most countries they report much lower levels of confidence in using computers than do high achievers. With the exception of a small number of countries their relative levels of comfort with and perceived ability to use computers are far below their relative level of interest in them (Figure 2.6).

| Figure 2.6 | Low achievers' interest in, comfort with and perceived ability to use computers, 2000[1] |

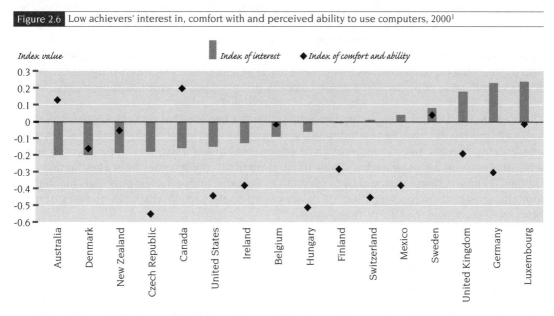

1. Each country's score on each of the indexes shows how low achievers in that country compare to the average for all students in the OECD. Both indexes are standardised to an OECD-wide mean of 0.0 and a standard deviation of 1.0. Values are arranged in order of low achievers' interest in computers.

Source: PISA database.

Data for Figure 2.6, p. 73.

Nevertheless some limited case study evidence suggests that motivational barriers to the use of ICT can be addressed, and that ICT can, in particular, be a tool for improving low achievers' interest in learning. Pelgrum (2004) reports that 10% of the case studies in the Second International Technology in Education Survey (SITESM2) contained evidence of a particular impact of ICT upon low ability students or students at risk. While quantitative evidence from SITESM2 does not throw much light upon whether ICT can help to fight low achievement, Pelgrum reports that case studies point to the frequency with which ICT use among low achievers is associated with improved motivation, self-esteem and self-confidence. For example the case studies report that use of ICT in learning can motivate weaker students by enabling them to present their work more neatly, revealing hidden strengths, tailoring instruction more closely to individual needs, providing more frequent feedback, and allowing them to work independently. Wilhelm (2004) similarly reports case studies in which the impact of ICT upon low achievers' motivation to learn appears to be more significant than its measured impact upon performance.

5. WHAT ARE THE BARRIERS TO ICT IMPROVING THE QUALITY OF TEACHING AND LEARNING?

Limited resources are a barrier to the more effective educational use of ICT in most OECD countries and are quite significant in some. For example ISUSS data show that in Ireland and Mexico school principals report that three quarters of all upper secondary students are affected by insufficient numbers of computers, and similar numbers of students by equipment that is outdated. Even countries such as Denmark and Norway, where computers in schools are more plentiful, report problems with insufficient or outdated equipment (OECD, 2004a, Table 3.16a).

The constraints that prevent ICT being used to improve the quality of teaching and learning are not a simple matter of the level of investment in hardware. They can also be a result, as pointed out above, of insufficient use of the hardware that is available. They can also be the result of the ways that ICT resource policies are phrased. For example where national ICT resource policies are directed to achieving targets such as a certain number of students per computer, or a given proportion of schools or classrooms connected to the Internet, individual schools may not be able to purchase other types of hardware that may allow a better and more creative integration of ICT into the teaching process – such as digital cameras, scanners or colour printers (Kugemann, 2002). A more flexible way of phrasing ICT resource policy priorities might avoid such problems.

These examples illustrate a more fundamental point: the barriers that prevent ICT being used as well as it could to improve the teaching and learning process are linked to the heart of the teaching and learning process, to the organisation of educational institutions, and to the ways in which education systems are organised. A simple illustration of this point comes from a key finding from the OECD's International Survey of Upper Secondary Schools. In that survey, principals highlighted four obstacles to them reaching their ICT development goals, each of which affected 60% or more of all students across the OECD. These were:

• Difficulty in integrating computers into classroom instruction.

• Problems in scheduling enough computer time.

• Teachers' lack of knowledge in using computers as a teaching tool.

• Teachers not having enough time to prepare lessons that use computers (OECD, 2004a, Table 3.16a).

These four problems are not likely to be resolved without addressing the timetable, teachers' knowledge and skills, and the allocation of time within schools. By itself, then, the introduction of

ICT into schools is unlikely to result in improved learning outcomes. The skills of the teacher and the organisation of the school are key factors that need to be tackled. Lack of teacher interest in ICT or teacher resistance to ICT do not seem to be the most important barriers: the ISUSS survey found that only around a third of students, in the countries surveyed, were in schools where this was reported to be an obstacle, compared to the two thirds who were in schools where difficulty in integrating computers into classroom instruction was reported to be a problem (OECD, 2004a, p. 124). A similar conclusion about teachers' ICT-related motivation emerges from analysis of the SITESM2 case studies (Pelgrum, 2002).

Certainly some OECD countries have been treating the ICT skills of teachers as a serious issue in recent years. They have invested considerable resources in providing computers for teachers to use, and in ICT training programmes for teachers. Box 2.1 above illustrates the extent of such programmes in the case of Korea and New Zealand. The OECD's ISUSS survey found that in all the countries surveyed except Belgium (Flemish Community), France and Italy, teachers had better access to computers than did students (OECD, 2004a, p. 79). It also found that in 2000-01 half of all Danish upper secondary teachers took part in ICT-related staff development activities, and that in Finland and Norway the proportion exceeded 40%.

Nevertheless it is reasonable to ask whether the type of ICT-related training that teachers are receiving is either sufficient or of an appropriate type. For example although in Denmark, Finland and Norway in 2000-01 high proportions of teachers received ICT-related training, Norwegian principals reported that 87% of upper secondary students attended schools where teachers' lack of knowledge or skills in using computers for instructional purposes was a barrier to the achievement of schools' ICT goals. In Denmark and Finland 59% and 66% respectively of upper secondary students attended schools where this was reported to be the case. So the nature, and not just the quantity, of the ICT-related training that teachers receive is clearly important if the potential of ICT to improve teaching and learning is to be realised. That training needs to go beyond the development of ICT skills to also focus heavily upon the pedagogical skills needed to integrate ICT into the curriculum and the classroom.

By itself training of an appropriate type will not result in more effective uses of ICT unless the organisational and structural barriers that exist within the school are also addressed. Box 2.3 gives an example of a comprehensive national programme to develop teachers' ICT skills which concentrated upon the development of pedagogical skills, and which also took account of the ways in which the schools are organised.

Box 2.3 Sweden's National Action Programme for ICT in Schools (ITiS)

During the four-year period 1999-2002 Sweden ran a very large programme to improve the quality of teaching and learning, costing some €190 million. ITiS was both an ICT project and a school development project. It had seven components:

- In-service training for 60 000 teachers in teams.
- A multimedia computer provided to all participating teachers.
- Funds to improve schools' Internet access.
- E-mail addresses for all teachers and all students.
- Funds to develop the Swedish Schoolnet and to support the European Schoolnet.
- Measures for students with special needs.
- Awards for excellent pedagogical contributions.

...

> The programme covered all schools: pre-school, compulsory and upper secondary. The content of the training was project-based, and topics were selected by teams of teachers within their own schools. Each team carried out an interdisciplinary problem-based pupil oriented development project together with its group of students. Nearly all training occurred within the school itself, with strong external support systems for teachers built in from external tutors, and associated training seminars for local school boards and school politicians.
>
> *Source*: Delegation for ICT in Schools (2002).

6. WHAT ARE THE OPPORTUNITIES FOR OVERCOMING THESE BARRIERS? LESSONS FROM INNOVATIVE SCHOOLS

Whatever the problems and barriers outlined above, an encouraging message from OECD work on ICT and education is that in all countries examples can be found of schools that have adopted an innovative approach to the use of ICT, and which have succeeded in integrating it into their teaching processes to improve students' learning. The OECD's Centre for Educational Research and Innovation (CERI) has conducted 94 case studies in 23 countries to understand how ICT relates to educational innovation (Venezky and Davis, 2002). The case studies illustrate the barriers that need to be overcome within the school if ICT is to improve students' learning, but more importantly they illustrate steps that can be and have been taken to surmount these barriers. The case studies are varied. For example they include a school in the United States that used ICT to facilitate the introduction of an inquiry-based learning programme, and a school in the Netherlands in which ICT was used to help the school move towards self-study. The level of technology introduced ranged from the development of a sophisticated intranet in a school in Singapore that allowed wide sharing of information on curriculum resources and extended the possibilities for communication between schools, parents and communities, to a school in Mexico that made innovative use of graphical calculators for teaching purposes.

One of the key questions explored by the case studies is whether ICT is itself a sufficient condition for educational innovation, or whether an innovative approach to teaching and learning is a precondition for the effective use of ICT. Several of the schools did report that the introduction of ICT had led to changes in pedagogy. For example a Finnish secondary school reported that it led to more student-centred learning, and that students became more active in collecting, processing and constructing information. Nevertheless in many other schools ICT proved to be not a catalyst for change, but an enabler of changes that had already been planned and decided. For example in one Irish primary school ICT was only one of the ways, along with a school play, music and other activities in which the school was extending more student-centred approaches to learning. In most cases ICT proved to be an enabling technology that helped the process of school reform. It provided opportunities for change. This was by far the more common experience. Box 2.4 illustrates this process in the case of two Australian schools.

For most of the case study schools, the adoption of ICT was not a single step, but an ongoing process. Teachers did not all adopt ICT simultaneously, but the use of ICT spread gradually through the teaching force. Thus the integration of ICT into teaching involves its adoption by individual teachers in the context of their own subject.

The case studies indicate that a number of factors are important in successfully implementing ICT so that it results in improved teaching and learning. No single factor determines success, but there are a number that may be present in varying degrees, depending upon circumstances.

Box 2.4 ICT in two innovative schools in Australia

Bendigo Senior Secondary College and Glen Waverley Secondary College are both public high schools in the State of Victoria in Australia. Over a three-to-five year period both decided to shift their curriculum delivery to be project-based, to emphasise student autonomy in learning, and to shift teaching from being teacher-centred to teacher-guided. School management and teacher planning teams set teaching and learning goals for their schools: for teachers, students and administrators. Continuous improvement is an important part of each school, and both regard themselves as learning organisations. Steps taken to reform the schools have included: revised management structures and decision-making processes to increase staff involvement; an expanded and revised curriculum; extensive professional development and an annual staff appraisal process; and a revised timetable and more flexible patterns of student access.

Both schools developed intranets for submission of student work and for student learning. The staff contribute lessons and support materials to their online systems. While ICT was a factor in some decisions, the emphasis on student autonomy was principally driven by pedagogical reasons, not ICT. Nevertheless, once integrated into the schools, ICT opened up further opportunities for innovation and the schools based their reforms upon a belief that well integrated ICT enhances teaching and learning.

Source: Toomey, EkinSmyth and Nicolson (2000).

Access to adequate technology was a prerequisite for successful adoption of ICT for improved teaching and learning. However with limited computer availability, some schools have given courses that develop ICT skills first priority in access, often leaving those teachers wanting to use ICT to improve their teaching practice with little or no access. Access to the Internet is of particular importance for schools. By providing access to the resources of the web, the Internet access can facilitate learning that is centred on student research. In addition Internet access enables a whole range of communication activities, including links with other schools, allowing parent access or allowing distance learning. However it was found to be important for access to the Internet to be fast and reliable, rather than delivered through slow dial-up connections, which were commonly found to be frustrating. A lack of suitable educational software was found to be a barrier to use of ICT in some cases. ICT use was further limited by problems with technical support. In most schools, technical difficulties were reported as a major barrier to usage, and a source of frustration for students and teachers. Where there were formal arrangements in place for providing technical support, the structures varied widely. Some schools reduced a teacher's workload slightly to allow time for technical work. In some cases full-time technical specialists were hired. Despite the variety of structures, the overwhelming view was that technical support was both inadequate and a major barrier to the development of ICT. The US corporate standard of a full-time technical support person for every 50 computers was beyond the wildest dreams of most schools.

But equipment and resources alone were not found to be enough: some very well-equipped schools found that few of their teachers made use of ICT. This finding focuses attention on the importance of teacher skills and attitudes. The case studies show that teachers need sufficient ICT skills to make use of the technology and to feel confident enough to use the technology in a classroom setting. But teachers also require insights into the pedagogical role of ICT, in order to find meaningful uses for the technology in their teaching. No matter what teachers' ICT skills, they need to see the educational potential of ICT. Almost all of the case study schools reported some staff development activities aimed at preparing teachers to use ICT. Many of the schools used peer-tutoring systems, where experienced ICT users were encouraged to act as mentors to teachers with less experience, and released from teaching duties to do so. In some cases the training was not provided in the school, which was experienced as a problem, in contrast to the in-school development models such as those found to be common in Denmark. Another problem with staff development models is that participation in training was often voluntary, thus reaching mainly those with an existing interest in ICT. And schools also stressed the importance of funding for release time. Box 2.3 illustrates a successful ICT staff development model that attempts to address these problems.

The case study schools highlighted a series of other factors that played an important role in the adoption of ICT. School leadership emerged as one of the key issues. A second major factor was the presence among the staff of an ICT champion. The curriculum was also a powerful factor. In schools, particularly where there are high-stakes examinations, the curriculum has a very strong role in steering the nature of the educational activity. Some countries reported that appropriate use of ICT was actively encouraged in curricular documents. Highlighting the potential of ICT within the existing curriculum is of course just part of the solution. If the aim of ICT implementation is to facilitate more problem solving and inquiry-based learning, curricula may have to be adapted to re-focus on these aims. Where education systems relied on examinations involving recall of a specific body of facts, the implementation of a student-centred educational reform using ICT was more problematic. Other factors found in case study schools that appeared to have successfully integrated ICT into their teaching were teacher release time, and adjustment to the timetable to allow for small group work or individual research.

7. CONCLUSION

The evidence reviewed in this chapter points to a number of barriers that are preventing countries from realising substantial educational benefits from their investments in ICT. These include inadequate levels of investment; insufficient use of the equipment that has been purchased; insufficient emphasis upon teacher development; and inappropriate teacher development. In many OECD countries learning is not a major focus of young people when they use computers.

Whilst the evidence from different sources is not always consistent, it seems as if only a limited number of OECD countries are in a position to gain significant educational benefits from their investments in educational ICT in schools, even though many individual schools within particular countries are at the forefront of innovation. Some of the Nordic countries, Australia and New Zealand are among the countries that appear to have made investments in educational ICT that are large enough to allow most students to gain access to the technology fairly frequently, and they are countries in which the technology does not appear to sit unused or to be infrequently used. In this group of countries investment in equipment has often been complemented by extensive teacher training, and patterns of computer use by young people, both within the school and outside it, more often point to uses that emphasise educational and learning purposes. In these countries one can also at times see an awareness of the importance of treating improved educational uses of ICT as a specific case of the general need to improve teaching and learning and to reform schools. A basic problem in gaining improved educational benefits from ICT, no matter how strong the benefits in terms of the production of ICT skills for the labour market and for everyday living, is that too frequently countries have seen it mainly as a technological issue, and not as an issue in school reform and school improvement.

Strikingly similar messages emerge from the OECD work on ICT in education that has been reviewed here and from OECD work on the relationship between investment in ICT and the productivity of firms (OECD, 2003a). In the case of business performance the message is very clear. By itself ICT does not necessarily raise productivity. In order to capitalise on the potential of ICT to improve productivity, firms need to innovate, changing the nature of their products and processes. Investment in ICT needs to be complemented by other investments such as changes in the organisation of work and changes in workers' skills. Installing ICT will not compensate for poor management, lack of skills, lack of competition or a low ability to innovate. It has been argued (Carnoy, 2002) that in business the most common use of ICT has been to increase productivity by analysing employee performance and working with employees to improve it. This form of management is highly underdeveloped in education, where the vast body of data on student performance available to schools is unused through lack of teacher and educational manager skills in using ICT for data based management. Improving such skills could make it easier for teachers not only to track the performance of their own students over time, but allow them to see the relationship between the introduction of certain practices and improvement in student performance. Such improvement in teacher capacity could be a promising future direction for improving the capacity of ICT to contribute to the quality of education.

References

Angrist, J. and V. Lavy (2002), "New Evidence on Classroom Computers and Pupil Learning", *The Economic Journal*, Vol. 112, October, pp. 735-765.

Archbald, D. (2001), "Information Technology and the Goals of Standards-based Instruction: Advances and Continuing Challenges", *Education Policy Analysis Archives*, Vol. 9, No. 48, *http://epaa.asu.edu/epaa/v9n48/*

BECTA (British Educational Communications and Technology Agency) (2002), "ImpaCT2 – The Impact of Information and Communication Technologies on Pupil Learning and Attainment", *www.becta.org.uk/research/*

Carnoy, M. (2002), "ICT in Education: Possibilities and Challenges", paper delivered at an OECD/Japan Seminar on "The Effectiveness of ICT in Schools: Current Trends and Future Prospects", Tokyo.

Castells, M. and P. Himanen (2002), *The Information Society and the Welfare State: The Finnish Model*, Oxford University Press, Oxford.

Cuban, L. (2001), *Oversold and Underused: Computers in the Classroom*, Harvard University Press, Harvard.

Delegation for ICT in Schools (2002), *The National Action Programme for ICT in Schools* ITIS 1998-2002, Ministry of Education and Science, Stockholm.

Green, F., A. Felstead and D. Gallie (2000), "Computers are even more Important than you Thought: An Analysis of the Changing Skill-intensity of Jobs", Discussion Paper No. 439, Centre for Economic Performance, University of London.

Kugemann, W. (2002), "ICT and Educational Resource Policy", paper delivered at an OECD/Japan Seminar on "The Effectiveness of ICT in Schools: Current Trends and Future Prospects", Tokyo.

Kulik, J. (2003), "Effects of Using Instructional Technology in Elementary and Secondary School: What Controlled Evaluation Studies Say", SRI International, Arlington, Va., *www.sri.com/policy/csted/reports/sandt/it/Kulik_ITinK-12_Main_Report.pdf*

Ministry of Education, Denmark (1998), *Information and Communication Technologies in the Education System: Action Plan for 1998-2003*, Copenhagen.

Ministry of Education, New Zealand (2002), Digital Horizons: Learning Through ICT. A Strategy for Schools, Auckland.

Ministry of Education and Human Resource Development and Korea Education and Research Information Service (2002), Adapting Education to the Information Age: A White Paper, Seoul.

National Center for Education Statistics (2001), "Internet Access in U.S. Public Schools and Classrooms: 1994-2000", Statistics in Brief, U.S. Department of Education, Office of Educational Research and Improvement, NCES 2001-071, May.

OECD (1999), "Technology in Education: Trends, Investment, Access and Use", Education Policy Analysis, OECD, Paris, pp. 47-64.

OECD (2001), Learning to Change: ICT in Schools, OECD, Paris.

OECD (2003a), ICTs and Economic Growth: Evidence from OECD Countries, Industries and Firms, OECD, Paris.

OECD (2003b), Beyond Rhetoric: Adult Learning Policies and Practices, OECD, Paris.

OECD (2004a), Completing the Foundations for Lifelong Learning: An OECD Survey of Upper Secondary Schools, OECD, Paris.

OECD (2004b), The Economic Impact of ICT: Measurement, Evidence and Implications, OECD, Paris.

OECD (2004c), Information Technology Outlook 2004, OECD, Paris.

Pelgrum, W. (2002), "Teachers, Teacher Policies and ICT", paper delivered at an OECD/Japan Seminar on "The Effectiveness of ICT in Schools: Current Trends and Future Prospects", Tokyo.

Pelgrum, H. (2004), "Promoting Equity through ICT: What can International Assessments Contribute to Help Fight Low Achievement?", in A. Kárpáti (ed.), Promoting Equity Through ICT in Education: Projects, Problems, Prospects, Hungarian Ministry of Education and OECD, pp. 13-55.

Pont, B. and R. Sweet (2003), "Adult Learning and ICT: How to Respond to the Diversity of Needs?", paper delivered at a joint OECD/National Center on Adult Literacy Roundtable on "ICT in Non-formal and Adult Education, Supporting Out-of-school Youth and Adults", November, University of Pennsylvania.

Selwyn, N. (2003), "ICT in Non-formal Youth and Adult Education: Defining the Territory", paper delivered at a joint OECD/National Center on Adult Literacy Roundtable on "ICT in Non-formal and Adult Education, Supporting Out-of-school Youth and Adults", November, University of Pennsylvania.

Sweet, R. and A. Meates (2004), "ICT and Low Achievers: What does PISA Tell us?", in A. Kárpáti (ed.), Promoting Equity Through ICT in Education: Projects, Problems, Prospects, Hungarian Ministry of Education and OECD, pp. 13-55 and www.pisa.oecd.org/docs/Further_reading.htm

Toomey, R., C. EkinSmyth and P. Nicolson (2000), "Case Studies of ICT and School Improvement at Bendigo Senior Secondary College and at Glen Waverley Secondary College", OECD/CERI Programme on ICT and the Quality of Learning, Victoria, Australia, www.oecd.org/edu/

Torgerson, C. and D. Zhu (2003), A Systematic Review and Meta-analysis of the Effectiveness of ICT on Literacy Learning in English, 5-16, EPPI Centre, eppi.ioe.ac.uk/EPPIWebContent/reel/review_groups/english/eng_rv2/eng_rv2.pdf

Venezky, R. and C. Davis (2002), "Quo Vademus? The Transformation of Schooling in a Networked World", OECD, Paris, www.oecd.org/edu/

Wilhelm, A.G. (2004), "Everyone Should Know the Basics: Equalizing Opportunities and Outcomes for Disadvantaged Youths through ICTs in Education", in A. Kárpáti (ed.), Promoting Equity Through ICT in Education: Projects, Problems, Prospects, Hungarian Ministry of Education and OECD, pp. 81-96.

Woo, S. and J. Pang (2002), "The Use of ICT for Learning: The Current Status and Future of the Republic of Korea", presented at a CMEC-OECD-Canada Seminar on Future Challenges in Education and ICT: Policy, Planning and Practice, Montreal, April.

Zemsky, R. and W.F. Massy (2004), "Why the E-learning Boom Went Bust", Chronicle of Higher Education, July 9, chronicle.com/prm/weekly/v50/i44/44b00601.htm

Data for Figure 2.1

Mean number of 15-year-old students per computer, 2003

	Mean number
United States	3
Australia	4
Hungary	4
Korea	4
New Zealand	4
United Kingdom	4
Austria	5
Canada	5
Denmark	5
Japan	5
Luxembourg	5
Finland	6
Iceland	6
Norway	6
Sweden	6
Switzerland	6
Belgium	7
Netherlands	7
Italy	8
Czech Republic	9
Ireland	9
Germany	12
Greece	12
Mexico	12
Spain	12
Portugal	14
Poland	15
Slovak Republic	15
Turkey	25

Source: PISA database.

Data for Figure 2.2

Students per computer and GDP per capita, 2003

	GDP per capita[1]	15-year-old students per computer
Australia	28 500	4
Austria	29 500	5
Belgium	28 400	7
Canada	31 000	5
Czech Republic	16 700	9
Denmark	29 800	5
Finland	27 400	6
Germany	26 300	12
Greece	19 500	12
Hungary	14 600	4
Iceland	29 800	6
Ireland	33 200	9
Italy	26 100	8
Japan	28 000	5
Korea	20 300	4
Luxembourg	50 900	5
Mexico	9 400	12
Netherlands	29 100	7
New Zealand	22 800	4
Norway	36 100	6
Poland	11 500	15
Portugal	18 400	14
Slovak Republic	13 000	15
Spain	23 200	12
Sweden	28 100	6
Switzerland	30 400	6
Turkey	6 800	25
United Kingdom	29 000	4
United States	37 600	3

1. In USD using purchasing power parities.
Source: PISA database and OECD.

Data for Figure 2.3

Percentage of upper secondary students attending schools with access to the Internet, 1995 and 2001

	1995	2001
Korea	7	100
Belgium (Fl.)	9	100
Mexico	9	76
France	12	99
Ireland	14	100
Spain	14	98
Italy	16	100
Hungary	18	100
Switzerland	20	99
Portugal	22	95
Norway	39	100
Sweden	43	91
Denmark	52	100
Finland	57	100

Source: OECD (2004a, Table 3.7).

Data for Figure 2.4

Average frequency with which 15-year-old students used computers at school, 2000 and 2003

	2000 index	2003 index	% change 2000-03
Denmark	2.7	2.8	6
United Kingdom	2.4	2.7	15
Hungary	2.5	2.7	10
Australia	2.3	2.6	11
Austria	m	2.4	m
Sweden	2.2	2.4	6
United States	2.0	2.3	14
New Zealand	1.9	2.2	18
Czech Republic	1.7	2.2	34
Iceland	m	2.2	m
Canada	m	2.2	m
Poland	m	2.1	m
Mexico	1.3	2.1	65
Finland	2.3	2.1	-6
Italy	m	2.1	m
Greece	m	2.0	m
Slovak Republic	m	2.0	m
Switzerland	1.6	1.9	14
Portugal	m	1.8	m
Belgium	1.7	1.7	0
Turkey	m	1.7	m
Japan	m	1.6	m
Korea	m	1.6	m
Germany	1.2	1.6	27
Ireland	1.5	1.5	-1

Note: A value of 0.0 on the index corresponds to "Never"; a value of 1 to "Less than once a month"; a value of 2 to "Between once a week and once a month"; a value of 3 to "A few times each week" and a value of 4 to "Almost every day".
Source: PISA database.

Data for Figure 2.5

Mean number of computers in the homes of the lowest and highest achievers, 2000

	Mean number of computers in the homes of 15-year-old students who on the PISA combined literacy scale scored at:	
	Level 1 and below	Levels 4 and 5
Mexico	0.12	0.76
Hungary	0.31	0.89
Greece	0.42	0.69
Poland	0.44	0.68
Portugal	0.45	1.05
Czech Republic	0.45	0.86
France	0.53	1.04
Spain	0.57	1.05
Ireland	0.72	0.90
Italy	0.74	0.98
Japan	0.76	1.10
Korea	0.76	1.05
United States	0.84	1.56
New Zealand	0.85	1.26
Belgium	0.89	1.44
Finland	0.90	1.21
Austria	0.97	1.38
Switzerland	1.02	1.53
Luxembourg	1.03	1.62
Germany	1.05	1.56
Canada	1.05	1.44
Australia	1.15	1.56
Sweden	1.30	1.71
Denmark	1.39	1.72
Norway	1.46	1.62
Netherlands	1.53	1.71
United Kingdom	1.55	1.56
Iceland	1.56	1.55

Source: PISA database.

Data for Figure 2.6

Low achievers' interest in, comfort with and perceived ability to use computers, 2000

	Index of interest	Index of comfort and ability
Australia	-0.20	0.12
Denmark	-0.20	-0.17
New Zealand	-0.19	-0.06
Czech Republic	-0.18	-0.56
Canada	-0.16	0.19
United States	-0.15	-0.45
Ireland	-0.13	-0.39
Belgium	-0.09	-0.02
Hungary	-0.06	-0.52
Finland	-0.01	-0.29
Switzerland	0.01	-0.46
Mexico	0.04	-0.39
Sweden	0.08	0.03
United Kingdom	0.18	-0.20
Germany	0.23	-0.31
Luxembourg	0.24	-0.02

Source: PISA database.

Chapter 3

HOW WELL DO SCHOOLS CONTRIBUTE TO LIFELONG LEARNING?

▼

SUMMARY

Lifelong learning means not just prolonging learning throughout life, but also ensuring that schooling prepares young people well for a life of learning. While most are now receiving the solid foundation of an upper secondary education, many have not acquired sufficient competences when they leave school. Education systems need to pay greater attention to improving broad cognitive and motivational outcomes of schooling. In doing so, schools will have to transform, ensuring that their staff are themselves lifelong learners, and that they become innovative as organisations to create more effective learning cultures centred around the perspective of the student. At the same time, education systems need to start asking themselves whether constant expansion focusing on the prolongation of initial education is the best route to lifelong learning, or whether it is making learning too "front-loaded" over the life course.

1. INTRODUCTION: SCHOOLING, THE NEGLECTED LINK IN THE LIFELONG LEARNING AGENDA

The ideal of lifelong learning originated as a strategy for continuing to educate people beyond their school years (OECD, 1973). More recently it has been promoted as a cradle-to-grave concept (OECD, 1996; OECD, 2001a) of which schooling is an early phase. This implies that school systems should have different objectives and characteristics than if education were considered to have been completed when a student leaves for adult and working life. Yet in practice, with a few exceptions (for example, Bryce *et al.*, 2000), there remains a tendency for school education to be assessed in terms of the achievements and targets that systems have set themselves, rather than their broader success in laying the foundation for lifelong learning. This chapter suggests a framework for making this broader assessment. It then applies this framework and uses OECD sources to provide an initial review of the extent to which schools are presently preparing students for lifelong learning.

Lifelong learning can mean different things to different people beyond its obvious reference to individuals of all ages continuing to learn. Some see this ambiguity as appropriate. Others see it as unhelpfully vague. While views differ about whether the concept of lifelong learning should be more precisely specified to give it greater value, its prominence has helped to shift basic assumptions about the nature of education in knowledge-intensive societies. It encapsulates a key idea: learning that is of significance to individuals and to communities must extend well beyond that which is organised through formal education systems; and it should certainly extend well beyond what takes place during childhood and youth. So strong has been the focus on continuing learning, however, that it is less clear that the full consequences of the cradle-to-grave perspective have been grasped; school policies still tend to be divorced from broader strategies aimed at promoting lifelong learning (for a fuller discussion see Istance, 2003).

2. A FRAMEWORK FOR PURSUING LIFELONG LEARNING IN SCHOOL SYSTEMS

In 2001, the OECD proposed four fundamental features of lifelong learning in general for consideration by Ministers of Education, which have implications for schooling in particular (OECD, 2001a, p. 11):

- Organised learning should be *systemic and inter-connected*. This implies that schooling should be an integral part of an overall education system, related coherently to other levels and types of learning. This systemic focus also raises the question of how education and training resources are distributed across the life cycle of each citizen.

- The learner should be *central to the learning process*. Educational policy discussions increasingly refer to this principle, using terms such as "the personalisation of learning". However, in practice putting the individual at centre-stage is a particularly challenging task in compulsory education compared with learning settings that more obviously incorporate personal choice.

- There should be an emphasis on *the motivation to learn*. This is critical, given the importance of maintaining inclusion for the least successful and of self-paced and individual regulation of learning that needs to continue throughout life.

- Recognition should be given to the *multiple objectives of education*. This argues for a need for balance, and it can be contrasted with a criticism that OECD formulations of lifelong learning give excessive weight to the economic rationale for learning and its instrumental ends.

Applying these features, a framework for assessing how well schooling promotes lifelong learning can be constructed at three levels: at the level of individual learners; at the level of schools, their organisation and their teaching practices; and at the level of school and education systems.

- *Students as learners*. Two main questions arise for a framework at this level: How widely does each school system develop the *competences* that support continued active learning throughout life, including "learning to learn"? How well does the experience of schooling *motivate* young people to continue learning? How well students are prepared for continued learning can thus be assessed in terms of the cognitive and non-cognitive qualities developed in young people, while recognising that schools are not uniquely responsible for developing them. To address these questions the chapter draws on results from PISA.

- *Schools, their organisation, and their teaching practices*. At this level, the key questions are: How far have schools adopted models that permit students to become flexible learners and that offer them an appropriately diverse curriculum and diverse assessment methods? And are teachers equipped to move towards these models? To address such questions about the development of learning the chapter draws upon results from several OECD studies of how teaching, knowledge and assessment are organised.

- *School and education systems*. Explicit attention needs to be given to how education in childhood and adolescence contributes to, and is balanced with, the whole range of learning opportunities over the life cycle. To address this, the chapter draws on various international indicators on the transition from school to working life.

The following sections provide a first assessment of how well school systems are performing on each of these three elements of the framework. This assessment is necessarily broad-brush, and cannot reflect the successes of, and challenges facing, specific systems.

3. STUDENTS AS LEARNERS – ESTABLISHING CAPACITIES FOR LIFETIMES OF LEARNING

How widely does each school system develop the competences that support continued active learning? The OECD's Programme for International Student Assessment (PISA) provides a rich source of data to help answer this question: it measures the degree to which 15-year-old students have mastered processes, understood concepts, and become capable of functioning in various situations (including learning situations) by applying reading, mathematical and scientific competences. "PISA focuses on things that 15-year-olds will need in their future lives and seeks to assess what they can do with what they have learned." (OECD, 2001b, p. 14). Scores reflect the aggregate effect of all influences in each country, not just school systems, and take a snapshot of student attributes at a single age; indeed, their precise predictive power of participation in education over the life cycle will only be known over the long haul using longitudinal studies. Nevertheless, it is clear that given the way that the PISA competences have been formulated, the results are highly pertinent to the question of how well young people coming to the end of their schooling are equipped for lifetimes of continued, often self-directed learning.

The domain covered in greatest detail in the PISA 2000 survey[1] was reading literacy. Students were assessed on their ability to retrieve information, to interpret texts, and to reflect on and evaluate texts. Student proficiency is measured for each of these individual aspects and for reading literacy overall. The results are assigned to one of six levels, from Level 5 (the highest) to below Level 1 (the lowest, indicating that students have failed to reach the first threshold of the skills that PISA seeks to measure). Level 3 can be taken as one benchmark of the reading competences required for meeting the demands of lifelong learning in rapidly-changing knowledge-intensive societies because those 15-year-olds who reach it are capable of reading tasks of moderate complexity, such

---

1. This was the first three-yearly PISA assessment. The results of the second assessment, in 2003, in which the focus was on mathematics, were published at the end of 2004.

as locating multiple pieces of information, making links between different parts of a text, and relating it to familiar everyday knowledge. Those who just fail to get to this level, but are proficient only at Level 2, are capable of basic reading tasks, such as locating straightforward information, making low-level inferences of various types, working out what a well-defined part of a text means, and using some outside knowledge to understand it (Box 3.1 provides definitions of all levels). This is not to define a sharp threshold between being prepared or not for lifelong learning but it is being proposed as a useful benchmark given the importance of making sense of unfamiliar information and using it in more complex ways.

Box 3.1 **Definition of levels on the PISA combined reading literacy scale**

Level 5   Students are capable of completing sophisticated reading tasks, such as managing information that is difficult to find in unfamiliar texts, showing detailed understanding of such texts and inferring which information in the text is relevant to the task; and being able to evaluate critically and build hypotheses, draw on specialised knowledge and accommodate concepts that may be contrary to expectations.

Level 4   Students are capable of difficult reading tasks, such as locating embedded information, construing meaning from nuances of language and critically evaluating a text.

Level 3   Students are capable of reading tasks of moderate complexity, such as locating multiple pieces of information, making links between different parts of a text, and relating it to familiar everyday knowledge.

Level 2   Students are capable of basic reading tasks, such as locating straightforward information, making low-level inferences of various types, working out what a well-defined part of a text means, and using some outside knowledge to understand it.

Level 1   Students are capable of completing only the least complex reading tasks developed for PISA, such as locating a single piece of information, identifying the main theme of a text or making a simple connection with everyday knowledge.

Below Level 1   Students are not capable of the most basic type of reading that PISA seeks to measure.

Source: OECD (2001b).

The results from the PISA assessments show wide differences across countries. Perhaps the most notable finding, for the purposes of this chapter, is the very large numbers in many countries who do not attain the Level 3 benchmark. In only ten of the OECD national educational systems surveyed in PISA 2000 do two-thirds of 15-year-olds reach the high minimum Level 3: Australia, Belgium (Flemish Community), Canada, Finland, Ireland, Japan, Korea, New Zealand, Sweden and the United Kingdom. In a further six OECD national educational systems, at least six in ten students reach this threshold. However in Belgium (French Community), the Czech Republic, Germany, Greece, Hungary, Italy, Luxembourg, Mexico, Poland, Portugal, Spain and Switzerland, fewer than 60% do so.

That fewer than six in ten teenagers approaching school-leaving age meet this high minimum of proficiency in so many OECD countries surveyed certainly raises the issue of how well schools are equipping most young people for lifetimes of learning. Clear variation also occurs between countries in the numbers with the very lowest proficiency. Fifteen per cent or more of students scored at best at Level 1 in as many as 18 of the 28 OECD national educational systems surveyed. In four of them, a quarter or more of all students fell into this group. Such students can at most complete the most basic of reading tasks in familiar settings. Skills at this level are unlikely to serve them adequately in life, or to help much with further study. Thus in the countries with significant numbers at these low levels, there are clear problems of young people leaving school seriously ill-equipped with the knowledge and skills to be lifelong learners.

| Figure 3.1 | 15-year-olds reaching specified thresholds on PISA combined reading literacy scale, 2000 (%) |

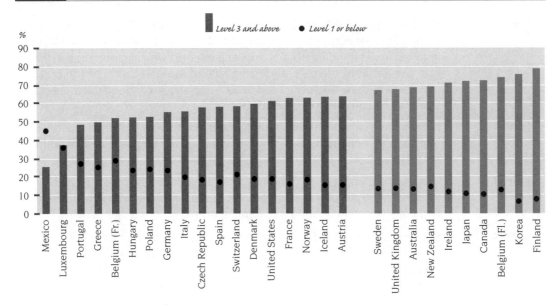

Notes: Countries are arranged in ascending order of the percentages of 15-year-olds scoring at Level 3 or above on the combined reading literacy scale.

Countries in which two thirds or more of 15-year-olds scored at Level 3 or higher and less than 15% scored at Level 1 or below are grouped separately on the right of the figure.

Turkey and the Slovak Republic did not participate in PISA 2000, and the Netherlands was excluded from certain comparisons because of a low response rate.

Source: OECD (2001b, Table 2.1a).

Data for Figure 3.1, p. 96.

Thus one measure of student capacity for lifelong learning can combine two indicators. The first of these, which should be maximised, is the proportion reaching or exceeding a high minimum benchmark on reading literacy: such as PISA Level 3. At this level students are capable of some of the complex and unfamiliar tasks that they will need in order to sustain learning beyond the structured environment of school. The second, which should be minimised, is the proportion which at best achieves the low minimum reading literacy benchmark of PISA Level 1 or below. Figure 3.1 illustrates how a few countries manage to get the great majority of their students above the high minimum, and at the same time to have only a small number who are at or below the low minimum. These countries are Australia, Belgium (Flemish Community), Canada, Finland, Ireland, Japan, Korea, New Zealand, Sweden and the United Kingdom.

As well as looking at how many students reach such thresholds, it is relevant to look at the distribution of students across the different levels of proficiency. Countries with high average performance on PISA can exhibit quite contrasting patterns of student proficiency and hence of preparedness for lifelong learning. Korea and New Zealand, for instance, both scored well overall compared with the OECD average of 500 points, with Korea at 525 and New Zealand at 529. Figure 3.2 shows that extremely few Korean students have very low proficiency, a smaller proportion than in any other country. Yet a relatively small proportion also performs at the highest Level 5, which is lower than in 18 of the other 28 OECD national educational systems covered. In New Zealand, more than three times as many students as in Korea are at Level 5 (19% compared to 6%) and this proportion is more than in any other country in the 2000 study. On the other hand, New Zealand also has over twice as many students with very low proficiency as Korea (14% compared to 6% at Level 1 or below). It is worth considering the different issues and challenges of such patterns of proficiency in laying the foundation for lifelong learning.

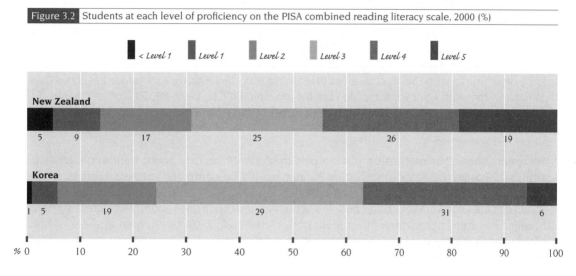

Figure 3.2 Students at each level of proficiency on the PISA combined reading literacy scale, 2000 (%)

Source: OECD (2001b, Table 2.1a).

Another measurable aspect of students' cognitive capacities is the strategies that they use for learning. (This is closely linked to their motivational characteristics, which are discussed below.) Analysis of students' learning strategies, as reported on the PISA questionnaire, shows that those who say that they adopt certain learning strategies have higher than average reading performance for that country. In particular, students who control their own learning, for example by checking that they have reached their learning goals, are likely to perform well. This is also a key requirement for becoming an autonomous learner throughout life. The survey also found that learning strategies differ somewhat for boys and for girls, with girls more likely to work out what they need to know, while boys are relatively strong in elaboration strategies and information processing (Artelt *et al.*, 2003).

Unfortunately, differences in the way that students in different cultures interpret questions make it possible to compare only a few such approaches to learning across countries. One type of learning strategy in PISA 2000 that is comparable across countries is the use of memorisation strategies. There seems no consistent pattern between these strategies and overall performance: in some countries with high scores (Australia, Ireland, New Zealand and Sweden, for instance) students use memorisation more than average while in others (for example Korea and Finland) they rely on it less. One hypothesis could be that, in a rapidly changing world, personal knowledge management strategies become increasingly important compared with abilities of recall. Another comparable feature of students' approaches to learning measured in PISA that is relevant to lifelong learning is how much they enjoy and engage in co-operative learning involving a team approach. In most countries the attitude of 15-year-olds is positive towards co-operation in learning, especially so in the United States, Denmark and Portugal. Students in Hungary and Korea, however, are "markedly negative" in their attitudes to co-operative learning and Hungarian students also rely more on memorisation than in other countries (Artelt *et al.*, 2003, p. 43). The different relationships involved would need much firmer evidence, however, before clear conclusions could be drawn about preparedness for lifelong learning.

4. STUDENTS AS LEARNERS – MOTIVATION AND ENGAGEMENT

One of the four fundamental features of lifelong learning identified in the framework of Section 2 is the emphasis on the motivation to learn. Learners will often need dogged determination to continue in the face of obstacles and the ability to identify opportunities when signposts are unclear, all of which calls for motivation. Schools are likely to influence whether students continue learning as much by fostering motivation as by generating knowledge and skills. The common story repeatedly told by older adults with the least interest in learning is of the negative experience of school days that has put them off education for life (see for example OECD, 1999; OECD, 2003e, Chapter 5). Fostering motivation and cognitive competence are not to be seen in opposition; ideally, the one should reinforce the other.

PISA results show that motivation plays a part in students' reports about their approaches to learning. Although aspects of motivation cannot readily be compared across countries, some findings about students' motivation, self-confidence and use of effective learning strategies are significant. One such finding is that only a few schools stand out in each country as fostering strong attitudes to learning across their full student body (Artelt *et al.*, 2003, p. 49): even where academic performance is strong, a school cannot take it for granted that all of its students are being well prepared to learn for life.

PISA has also generated important findings on students' more general motivation and their engagement at school (OECD, 2001b; OECD, 2002). The findings are in general positive. Contrary to the common image of teenagers as generally disengaged from their schools as alien or irrelevant environments, approximately three quarters of 15-year-olds across OECD countries as a whole reported in 2000 that they agree or strongly agree with the statement "I feel like I belong" at school. The proportion rises to 85% or more in certain countries such as Australia, Austria, Finland, Hungary, Iceland and Mexico. Asked whether they feel "awkward and out of place", only around one in seven students in most OECD countries agreed, and fewer than one in ten in the Czech Republic, Hungary, Ireland, Italy, Sweden and the United Kingdom. Even lower proportions state that they agree or strongly agree that "I feel like an outsider (or left out of things)". Fewer than one in ten described themselves in this bleak situation on average in OECD countries, and only between 5 and 6% did so in Denmark, Finland, Germany, Japan, the Netherlands, Norway, Spain and Sweden.

While positive attitudes reflect the role that schools play as centres of friendship and peer group contact, as well as their role as welcoming or stimulating learning environments, such evidence sheds a positive light on schooling in its relationship to lifelong learning. It would be hard for schools to lay a firm motivational basis for later learning if a high proportion of students felt they did not belong there. All is not positive, however. Even a relatively small minority of teenagers reporting negative attitudes is of concern, representing hundreds of thousands of students who do not connect with school. Moreover, in some countries, the proportion is not so small. Around one student in five reports feeling out of place in Austria, Belgium, Japan, Luxembourg and Portugal.

The OECD's analysis has developed an overall index of students' sense of belonging at school. This index combines the answers to six different questions about belonging at school (see Box 3.2). Figure 3.3 shows how many students in each country have relatively low scores on this index. A striking result is that in two of the three countries where a sense of belonging is lowest (Japan and Korea) students have some of the highest performance in reading, mathematical and scientific literacy. They also have some of the lowest rates of school absenteeism, as measured in PISA. So students in these countries appear to attend school, and perform well there, even though they feel least attuned to it as an environment. It is also hard to explain why in Sweden, where adults have high levels of measured competence and participation in learning[2] and where students in PISA expressed a high sense of belonging at school, they also reported a high level of absenteeism. Thus it appears that attitudes towards one's school environment do not translate directly into performance or attendance, since various cultural and socio-economic factors intervene to mediate these relationships. The lack of consistent patterns reinforces the need to use a broad range of outcomes to assess the enduring impact of education.

Box 3.2 Students' overall "sense of belonging"

Students were asked whether they strongly agreed, agreed, disagreed or strongly disagreed, in each case that: school is a place where:

a) I feel like an outsider (or left out of things).

b) I make friends easily.

c) I feel like I belong.

d) I feel awkward and out of place.

e) Other students seem to like me.

f) I feel lonely.

Figure 3.3 Students with a low sense of belonging at school, 2000 (%)

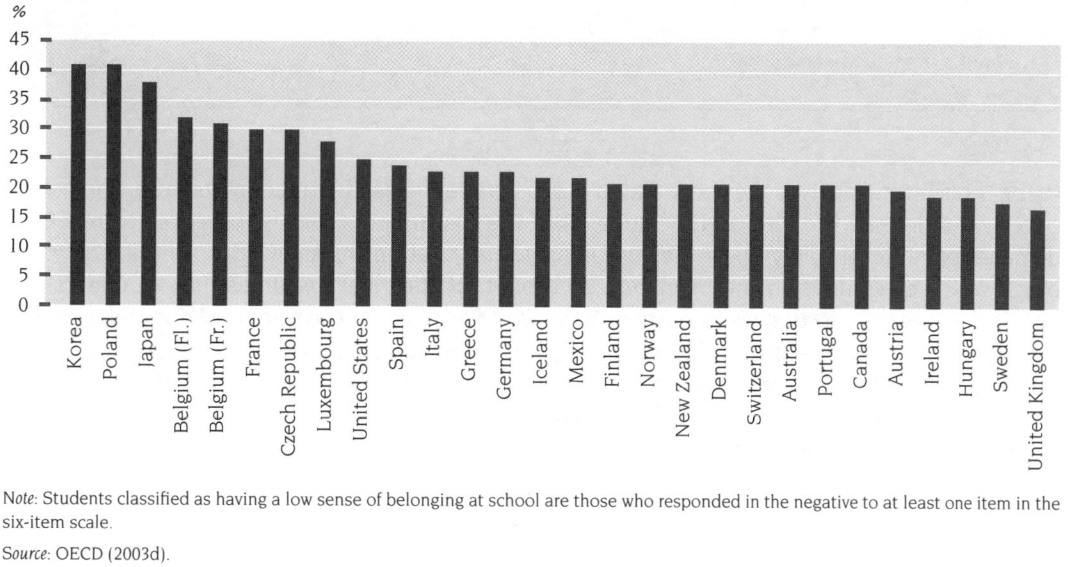

Note: Students classified as having a low sense of belonging at school are those who responded in the negative to at least one item in the six-item scale.

Source: OECD (2003d).

Data for Figure 3.3, p. 96.

---

2 . As measured on the International Adult Literacy Survey (OECD, 2000d).

One aspect of lifelong learning as a guiding concept mentioned at the outset is its openness – for some, vagueness – about the content of learning which relates to both the cognitive and non-cognitive. Implementation demands that attention be paid to content in ways that are not defined by any particular school curriculum. A useful point of departure for considering how the curriculum should support lifelong learning is the key competences developed through OECD's DeSeCo (Definition and Selection of Competences) project.[3] These competences are not just concerned with what goes on in school, but they do offer a way to assess the curriculum and the outcomes of education against broader objectives informed by lifelong learning objectives (Rychen and Salganik, 2003).

The fundamental competences identified by DeSeCo fall in three areas. The first is the ability to act autonomously. In turn, this incorporates two central ideas: the development of personal identity; and the exercise of autonomy in decision-making and choice. The abilities involved enable and empower a sense of self, the exercise of rights, and the assumption of responsibilities in different spheres of life. They require people to have an orientation toward the future and an awareness and understanding of their environment. Further details are listed in Box 3.3.

Box 3.3 Key competences for acting autonomously

- *The ability to defend and assert one's rights, interests, limits and needs*: this empowers people to put themselves forward and make choices as citizens, family members, workers, and consumers.

- *The ability to form and conduct life plans and personal projects*: this enables people to set goals that make sense in their lives and that are consistent with their values, and to achieve these goals.

- *The ability to act within the larger context*: this calls for people to understand the functioning of their larger context, their position in it, and for their behaviour to be informed by the possible consequences of their actions.

Source: Rychen and Salganik (2003).

Using tools interactively is the second area of key competences identified by DeSeCo. The notion of a tool is defined broadly, and includes all of the instruments that help people to meet the demands of modern society. These include language, information and knowledge, as well as physical objects such as computers and machines. To use a tool effectively assumes that we understand how it changes the way that we interact with the world around us. The third core competence area identified by DeSeCo is functioning in socially heterogeneous groups. Being dependent on and having ties to others, people need to be able to interact with those with different personalities and backgrounds. The specific DeSeCo formulations in this case concern the ability to relate to others, to co-operate, and to manage and resolve conflict.

---

3. DeSeCo was established at the end of 1997 as an international programme under OECD to meet the need for an explicit overarching conceptual framework to guide diverse work on competence and its measurement. DeSeCo's focus is on competences that matter both at the individual and societal level and in working life as well as life outside of work. The analysis and reflection in DeSeCo have not been restricted to what can be learned and taught in schools nor to what is readily measurable in large-scale assessments.

Such competence areas are not proposed as programmes or school curricula, and many will be acquired through a diffuse process combining formal and non-formal learning. The formulation of such competences does serve as a set of guidelines in this context to stimulate the question: "How well are these key competences promoted, directly or indirectly, through our schools?". Together with the measures developed through the PISA programme, they provide a valuable battery of reference points on progress towards lifelong learning.

5. SCHOOL ORGANISATION AND KNOWLEDGE MANAGEMENT

As an integral part of the overall range of learning opportunities, schools need to share the fundamental features of lifelong learning that were outlined at the beginning of this chapter: in particular they must become learner-centred. Many studies have argued for more flexible, open forms of learning and of school organisation but while it is not difficult to identify numerous promising examples, more sustained and widespread change is far less common. A variety of the factors inhibiting fundamental change to traditional practices has been analysed in OECD's Centre for Educational Research and Innovation (CERI) work on knowledge management (OECD, 2000b; OECD, 2003b; OECD, 2004a). In general, schools have weak networking and knowledge-sharing among teachers. Spending on educational research and development is very low and its application is quite limited. Most of the professional knowledge that teachers use in their daily work is tacit: it is rarely made explicit or shared with colleagues. Schools and classrooms are normally isolated one from another rather than interlinked. In short, schools still tend to have only rudimentary knowledge management practices, despite knowledge being education's explicit business.

The OECD's latest analysis of knowledge management in education (OECD, 2004a) identifies four key "pumps of innovation" which reveal shortcomings in realising innovative potential in the education sector:

- The first pump is *science-based innovation*. Education has not traditionally made much direct use of research knowledge, and the analysis suggests that there may be cultural resistance to doing so.

- The second pump is *collaboration between users and doers – horizontally organised innovation*. Here, there are obvious benefits in terms of teachers pooling their knowledge through networks, but incentives to do so remain underdeveloped.

- The third pump is *modular structures, with freedom to innovate yet joined together as a whole system*. Here, there are tensions between central and devolved control over the content and methods of education. A key problem occurs when the curriculum is presented as a static set of guidelines rather than a dynamic and evolving technique.

- The fourth pump is *information and communication technologies*. There is a powerful potential for ICT to transform education, but its use in schools remains underdeveloped, partly because the main *modus operandi* of school administration and instruction are highly resistant to change.

Despite such problems, there are signs of change. For example in relation to the first of the above innovation pumps, there is a growing attention to educational research and development (OECD, 2003b; OECD, 2004a). There is also a growing and related focus on decision-making that is informed by a robust evidence base. Furthermore networking is an emerging form of practice, of professional development and of governance (OECD, 2003a). Modularity is a familiar feature of educational organisation but what is really critical is what takes place at the interfaces – how connections are made and innovation generalised within systems – as much as within discrete units. School systems will innovate at the interfaces the more that they overcome the forms of bureaucracy that stifle innovation. In so doing, however, those responsible for making connections and generalising innovation become increasingly diffuse, and indeed the very notion of a "system" itself diffuses. So while the need for a systemic approach appears to be fundamental to lifelong learning, this begs the question of who initiates reform and co-ordinates it when responsibilities are widely diffused.

The fourth innovation pump, ICT, is regarded as especially important in this analysis as a source of information creation and of new modes of knowledge production. It can diminish the restraints of physical proximity, promote the benefits of scale, and act as a powerful motor for collective action. ICT in education is the subject of its own chapter in this volume. It is an area of major investments by school systems across OECD countries so that, as with modularity, there are signs of change as regards this source of innovation. But even within upper secondary education, where the indicators show high ICT investments, the International Survey of Upper Secondary Schools (ISUSS) for school year 2000-01 found that "… the educational use of computers is still sporadic in all participating countries. Computers are mostly used to obtain information from the Internet" (OECD, 2004b, p. 134). The CERI report *Learning to Change – ICT in Schools* (OECD, 2001c), echoes this message. It suggested that powerful tensions exist between traditional curricula and teaching strategies and the open, skills-based, student-centred approaches that can potentially be supported by ICT: "Dominant curricular and organisational patterns in school were not designed for the Internet age, and often inhibit its effective use." (OECD, 2001c, p. 15) Carnoy's (2002) analysis for the OECD of ICT use in education concludes that there is much that might be done, using ICT, to improve teacher knowledge, to improve the ways that information about student progress is shared among teachers, and to improve teaching strategies to respond to diverse learning needs.

Teachers are central to the success of schools in fostering lifelong learning. Where serious teacher shortages exist, efforts by schools to do more than in the past to prepare students for a life of learning in dynamic, flexible organisations are clearly at risk. The OECD study, *Teachers Matter: Attracting, Developing and Retaining Effective Teachers* (OECD, 2005a) has found marked differences among countries in reported teacher shortages. These are critical in some countries, particularly in high-demand subject areas such as mathematics. However they are non-existent in others such as Austria, Korea and Portugal, which enjoy a plentiful pool of candidates from which to draw. In all, about half of OECD countries have reported such shortages.

The study has consistently emphasised, however, that improved teaching should not be seen narrowly as a quantitative matter. It is essentially about the specific qualities, as well as the overall quality, of those coming into and remaining in the teaching force (OECD, 2005a; OECD, 2004c). Stressing the importance of quality immediately invites the question of what quality means. It must refer to more than simply the possession of advanced tertiary qualifications, however desirable they may be. It is also about the attitudes and professionalism that teachers bring to the job and develop during their careers. The literature is replete with lists of criteria for effective and high quality teaching. These include the ability to create a climate of mutually reinforcing high expectations; the ability to create positive student-centred learning environments with frequent feedback; and the ability to engage in intensive collaboration with colleagues. The challenge in developing teacher skills and professionalism consistent with lifelong learning may well be less to develop new criteria, than to ensure that they are the norm rather than exceptional practice across whole school systems. The organisation of schools as learning organisations and the fostering of such practices collectively are at least as important as the capabilities of individual teachers.

Central to both the collective professionalism of the teaching force and individual capabilities is the capacity to learn. There is no fixed definition of professional development, which in any case covers only one form of teacher learning. That said, continuing professional development, like initial training and induction, plays a critical role in establishing how teachers view their

| Figure 3.4 | Upper secondary teachers who participated in professional development activities in the 2000-01 school year, according to principals (%) |

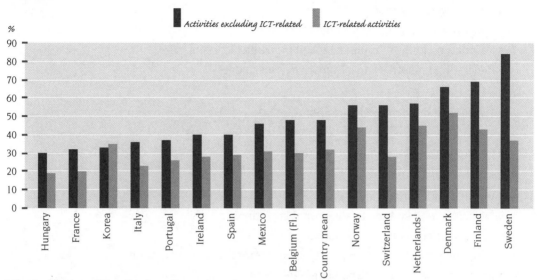

1. Country did not meet international sampling requirements.
Source: OECD (2004b), Table 3.12.

Data for Figure 3.4, p. 97.

professionalism and the educational challenges they will be facing. And the evidence shows that the extent to which teachers engage in professional development is very diverse across countries, as well as within them. The 2000 PISA survey indicated that on average across the surveyed countries principals report that around 40% of teachers attended a programme of professional development. This varied very widely, however: from less than 10% in Greece to 70% in New Zealand.[4] This finding is mirrored by the OECD Survey of Upper Secondary Schools (see Figure 3.4). Also based on principals' reports, this found very wide differences in teacher participation in professional development activities over the 2000-01 school year. The percentages of teachers who were reported to have participated varied from a high of over 80% in Sweden to under a third in Hungary (OECD, 2004b).

Teachers' continuous learning is influenced by the extent and nature of their professional collaboration, as well as by discrete professional development events. The structuring of their careers also strongly influences the continuous learning that teachers engage in. It is through exposure to different environments and challenges that teachers continue to learn. A major conclusion emerging from OECD work on attracting, retaining and developing effective teachers is that the career remains for the most part excessively flat and undifferentiated. In most countries there are insufficient opportunities and incentives for teachers to build careers that reflect their developing skills, performance and responsibilities. The existence of such career patterns would help to define teacher competences as part of a lifelong learning continuum. At the same time, there is general agreement that the demands made on teachers have widened and the OECD study has organised these into the framework presented in Box 3.4. Such demands are broadly consistent with the lifelong learning agenda such that the success of schools in meeting this agenda is highly dependent on the capacity of teachers in these different domains.

---

4. The New Zealand figure may have been unusually high, however, because of the introduction of new qualifications at the time of the survey.

Box 3.4 The broadening scope of teacher responsibilities

At *the individual student level*:
- Initiating and managing learning processes.
- Responding to the learning needs of individual learners.
- Integrating formative and summative assessment.

At *the classroom level*:
- Teaching in multicultural classrooms.
- Creating new cross-curricular emphases.
- Integrating students with special needs.

At *the school level*:
- Working and planning in teams.
- Evaluating and systematically improving planning.
- Using ICT in teaching and administration.
- Initiating projects between schools and international co-operation.
- Improving management and shared leadership.

At *the level of parents and the wider community*:
- Providing personal advice to parents.
- Building community partnerships for learning.

Source: OECD (2005a), pp. 87-88.

The intensive use of formative assessment of students and, just as critically, its use to shape teaching, are part of a more demanding definition of professionalism and have been studied in the most recent OECD/CERI "What Works in Innovation in Education" series (OECD, 2005b, which includes literature reviews relating to English-, French-, and German-language research). Formative assessment approaches[5] have been shown to be associated with very significant learning gains. Black and Wiliam (1998, p. 61) argue that "… the gains in achievement appear to be quite considerable … and among the largest ever reported for educational interventions". As well as promising to raise standards, such approaches address equity head on. They do so through the individualisation of teaching and learning strategies and through the continual identification of, and responses to, students who are experiencing difficulties. Moreover, these approaches are explicitly about developing cultures of learning in schools and classrooms. For all of these reasons, they are critical for lifelong learning. At the same time, they receive far less prominence than conventional forms of assessment such as achievement tests and examinations. Indeed the promotion of formative approaches may be inhibited by undue attention to such high-profile tests. Like the other directions for change discussed in this section, the adoption of formative assessment makes high demands upon teacher professionalism and school organisation as an integral part of the reform and lifelong learning agenda for schools.

---

5. Formative assessment refers to assessment of student progress that is an ongoing part of everyday teaching, rather than a special event. Formative assessment is designed to provide teachers and students with information about students' learning needs. It is designed to help students to assess their progress towards learning goals, and to help teachers to change and improve their teaching. It can include data from a number of sources such as classroom interactions, as well as more conventional forms of assessment such as tests and examinations.

Just as it is important to identify learning *needs* through formative assessment, so also it is critical to map out learning *routes* through effective guidance and information services. This becomes increasingly important as learning follows a continual and sometimes complex set of individualised pathways through initial schooling and beyond. It becomes even more obvious as countries pursue demand-led, as opposed to supply-driven models of provision. How adequate are these systems to meet the needs of all pupils and students, and how well adapted to the challenges of lifelong learning? The recent OECD review of career guidance policies found that much remains to be done (OECD, 2003c; OECD, 2004d). It welcomed a general tendency for guidance to be increasingly embedded within the school curriculum in OECD countries as a step towards an integrated approach to lifelong learning, rather than guidance issues being raised in an isolated way when schooling is nearly complete. However the analysis suggests that a broader approach is required, one much more explicitly tied to a lifelong learning agenda: "… at the least, career guidance services need to broaden from largely providing assistance with *decisions* at limited and selected points in people's lives to an approach which also encompasses the development of career-management *skills*." (OECD, 2003c, p. 25)

The powerful weight of traditional school organisation may thus impede the change that is desirable if schools are to offer the highly professional, learner-centred environments necessary for laying the basis for lifetimes of learning. A positive message from OECD work is that there are numerous excellent examples to draw on which show that change is possible. However school systems are very large and complex undertakings and the challenge is how such reform can be generalised and sustained across the board. The scenarios for the future of schooling developed by OECD (2001d, 2003a) reflect these differences in particular in the contrast between the bureaucratic "status quo" scenario and what are described as "re-schooling" futures (the "de-schooling" scenarios – which may also be consistent with lifelong learning – would instead witness an extensive dismantling of existing strong school systems). The shifts described in this section would be consistent with the emergence of the "re-schooling" scenario entitled "schools as focused learning organisations". More radical still is the other "re-schooling" model described as "schools as core social centres", in which the boundaries blur between schools and teachers, on the one hand, and communities, groups, and other professionals, on the other. This could provide a powerful platform for lifelong learning, both as education and other organisations share the same facilities and as the different generations come into much closer interaction.

6. SCHOOLING AND THE BROADER LIFE CYCLE DISTRIBUTION OF LEARNING OPPORTUNITIES

The first fundamental feature of lifelong learning outlined at the beginning of this chapter argues the need for a systemic and inter-connected approach to the way that learning is organised, rather than a fragmented approach in which policies for each educational sector are made separately. This calls for attention to how schooling fits into the whole initial education and training system. It also requires schooling to be seen in the context of the distribution of opportunities to learn over the entire life cycle. Yet serious consideration of the whole, as well as of the parts, of the education and training system is surprisingly rare. It requires careful thought to be given to the criteria by which progress towards learning societies is assessed. Such an exercise may sit uncomfortably with simple quantitative targets for more participation and longer duration of studies. It would need to recognise alternative forms of education. It would also need to recognise the possibility of a shorter duration of initial education alongside opportunities to return to learning at different points in the life cycle. Such an approach to target-setting is more complex but will be more appropriate to assessing progress towards lifelong learning.

When the early lifelong learning proposals emerged three decades or more ago, many proponents predicted that the front end model of education, concentrated in the early years of childhood and in adolescence, would fade away. Parallel predictions were made by radical de-schoolers at that time about the limited future of the school as an institution. Neither prediction has stood up well to the test of time. Education has become an even higher priority on political agendas, and participation in front end initial education systems continues to rise (see below). Indeed, the length of time that the young stay in initial education is widely interpreted as a positive indicator. Commentators often compare countries not only in terms of assessments of measured competences such as PISA or qualifications gained but also in terms of participation rates by age of people in their late teens or early 20s as if duration of initial studies by itself is synonymous with progress towards knowledge-based and learning societies.

There are, however, good reasons at least to examine the "more-of-the-same" assumptions that unquestioningly support ever-lengthening careers in initial education (see Schuller, Schuetze and Istance, 2002). There are social and cultural concerns about delaying the attainment of adulthood, and what this means for the healthy development of individuals and society as a whole. An important question that needs to be addressed is how the interest of many young people in learning, those with lowest motivation and achievement, can be maintained if the expected duration of initial education is continually pushed outwards and seemingly beyond grasp. The irony is that the goals of educational inclusion may be undermined by the front end expansion of systems that aims to promote these goals. Financing questions and issues of the affordability of very extensive periods of initial education, stretching from early childhood education through to tertiary education, are equally relevant to the argument. Such issues are particularly relevant as public expenditure is under intense pressure in most OECD countries. In ageing societies with pension bills growing steeply, lengthening periods of initial education help to increase dependency ratios, squeezing the active generation into an ever-tighter age range in the middle of people's lives. The sustainability of this trend is an urgent issue[6] (see also Duval, 2003).

In raising these questions, and reconsidering whether more participation in education by young adults is always better, the evidence relating to front end expansion and its interpretation needs to be carefully considered. Already by 2000, OECD analysis of transitions from school to working life suggested that between 1990 and 1996 the duration of young people's transition from initial education to working life grew by an international average of nearly two years (see OECD, 2000c). Now, nearly four-fifths of the 15-19 population across the OECD are students (79.4%), and in eight countries (Belgium, the Czech Republic, Finland, France, Germany, the Netherlands, Poland and Sweden) 85% or more are enrolled. The proportion of 20-to-29-year-olds who are students stands at over one in five for the OECD as a whole (22.7%), and over one in three in Australia, Denmark, Finland, Iceland and Sweden (OECD, 2004e, Table C1.2).

Another way to look at this question is through the lens of the expected career of the average 15-year-old, looking out over the next 15 years.[7] Within living memory, the age of 15 marked the end of education for the majority of the population. At the beginning of the 21st century, taking OECD countries and males and females together, the average 15-year-old can expect to spend as much time up to the age of 30 in education (6.4 years) as in employment (also 6.4) (OECD, 2004e, Table C4.1a).[8] Figure 3.5 shows that in thirteen OECD countries, the number of years that a 15-year-old can expect

---

6. OECD health data show that life expectancy at age 65 continued to grow for both men and women in all OECD countries over the decade 1991 to 2001 (OECD, 2004g, pp. 10-11). At the same time, the sustainability of retirement patterns for older workers is expressed in uncompromising terms on the OECD's web pages for employment: "one of the striking paradoxes of today's OECD societies is that although people live longer, they also tend to retire earlier – a situation which is clearly unsustainable from both the economic and social points of view."

7. Based on current enrolment patterns, rather than upon predictions about what might happen to participation rates up to 2020. Such patterns may be sensitive to unemployment rates.

8. The remaining 2.2 years can be expected to be spent either unemployed or out of the labour market altogether.

| Figure 3.5 | Expected years in education and not in education for 15-to-29-year-olds, 2002 |

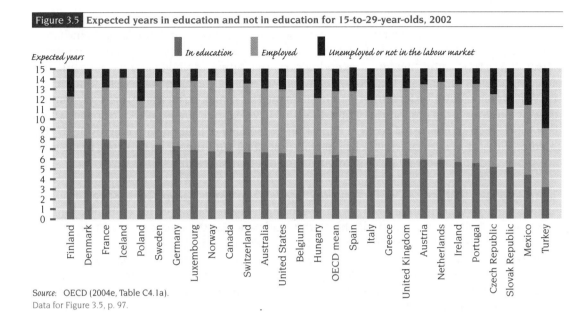

Source: OECD (2004e, Table C4.1a).
Data for Figure 3.5, p. 97.

to spend in education by the age of 30 exceeds the number of years expected to be spent in employment. In Finland and Poland, today's 15-year-olds can expect to spend only around half as much time in employment as in education before they turn 30. In France, the expected time in employment represents only around two thirds of that spent in education, and in Denmark and Iceland it is about three quarters of the time in education. As these are averages for the whole age group, they understate the extent to which the well-qualified are spending so much of the first three decades of their lives in education.

| Figure 3.6 | Expected years in education before age 30 of 15-year-olds (2002) and percentage of time in education expected to be combined with employment |

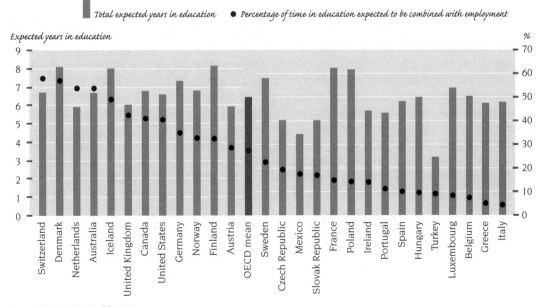

Source: OECD (2004e, Table C4.1a).
Data for Figure 3.6, p. 98.

The increased participation in education that can be expected by today's 15-year-olds up to the age of 30 could be the result of two factors: an extension of the period of initial education including increased participation in tertiary education after the end of school or a growing habit of returning to learning at times after this initial period is over. The latter possibility could be regarded as providing a welcome degree of flexibility and diversity of experience for young people, which might strengthen their motivation for further learning later on. This cannot be measured precisely, but one relevant indicator is the proportion of time that 15-to-29-year-olds are expected to spend, within their total expected number of years in education, combining education with employment. This could be either through: part-time jobs plus full-time study; full-time jobs plus part-time study; or through structured work-study programmes such as apprenticeships.[9]

Figure 3.6 shows that across OECD countries, today's 15-year-olds can expect to spend around a quarter of the 6.4 years that they will spend in education before the age of 30 combining learning with work. In Switzerland, Denmark, the Netherlands and Australia, over half of this time in education will be combined with working. On the other hand today's young people in Spain, Hungary, Turkey, Luxembourg, Belgium, Greece and Italy can expect to combine hardly any of their time in education with work. Such differences underline just how varied internationally are the patterns of experiencing adolescence and early adulthood: there is little evidence of convergence to an international norm.

If there is to be a re-examination of the continual extension of the initial education systems, including what this might mean for schools as well as for tertiary education, this should not undermine advances that are delivering a strong initial foundation to most of the young population as seen, for instance, in the completion of upper secondary education. Three-quarters of 25-to-34-year-olds have done so across OECD countries as a whole, and in several countries it is over 90%. The quest for better ways to lay a foundation for learning throughout life, however, need not jeopardise gains. The challenge is to explore alternative ways of sustaining progress towards learning societies without the financial and other costs associated with the continual expansion of initial education systems post-school. The exploration of such alternatives immediately raises questions about provision from the earliest years up to the end of the secondary cycle.

One key set of questions concerns how more can be done to develop schools as learning organisations in ways that are consistent with lifelong learning. Another set concerns the tight linkages that exist, and which underpin the structural organisation of school systems, between the age of the student and progression through the school cycle. Might much more flexibility be introduced into these linkages in order to create personalised learning pathways during the compulsory school cycles? As schools move nearer to becoming learning organisations, and as quality gains bear fruit, this might well open up the prospect of increasing numbers of students moving on to the upper secondary level at younger ages – one, two or three years before the conventional age – before then progressing to tertiary studies directly or experiencing other civic or employment activities. Hence reducing the dominance of a front-end focus is about changes in schooling towards greater flexibility and productivity, and the increased engagement in learning of those in the compulsory years, as well as changes at the post-compulsory and tertiary levels.

If searching questions are to be asked about the established structural patterns of schooling, this could well include review of the main cycles – primary, lower and upper secondary – that so powerfully define the school career and institutional structures at present. So extensive have been the changes in participation and attainment at the upper secondary and tertiary levels, that such

---

9. Another indicator, not reflected in this measure, of flexible activity patterns during late adolescence would be a measure of the periods spent alternating between work, education and other activities.

ingrained features of the educational landscape might need themselves to be scrutinised. One avenue for exploration is whether the hard demarcation between primary and secondary schooling should be substantially blurred, with these levels integrated into a shorter cycle of uniformly intense and high quality provision. This might then serve as a platform for highly diversified, even "de-schooled" opportunities along pathways combining education, work and a variety of other civic and social activities. As tertiary education is already becoming a mass experience, should its conventional starting age and its relationship to upper secondary programmes now be thoroughly reviewed? A broad lifelong learning focus, as opposed to fragmented sectoral perspectives, stimulates the posing of such larger questions.

7. CONCLUSION

This chapter has argued that the ways in which schools can and should contribute to the overall enterprise of lifelong learning have been seriously neglected, in international and even national discussions. Using existing OECD analyses, the chapter has presented a three-level framework for assessing how schools are laying the foundations for lifelong learning. The framework is at the level of:

- School students as learners, focusing upon the competences and motivation acquired for lifetimes in learning.

- The organisation of schools and of their teaching practices.

- School systems, and of how schooling fits into initial education and training systems and the wider distribution of educational opportunities over the life cycle.

The chapter arrives at both positive and negative conclusions about the contribution that schools are making to lifelong learning. On the positive side, upper secondary attainment levels are very high in many countries, and schools tend to be judged positively by young people as places where they feel they belong, even among teenagers of an age when they might most feel alienated from them. Another positive conclusion is that combining education and employment has become a normal part of the transition from school to adult life in a number of countries, which may often bring flexibility to pathways and choices in line with a less rigid demarcation between initial and continuing education. And finally, there are a number of the key changes to transform schools more systematically into learning organisations: networking, professional development, individualised learning assessment and responsive teaching strategies, R&D, and the exploitation of ICT by schools and educational management. Reform agendas for schools have permitted many of these changes to move from the margins into more mainstream policy discussion.

But there are also less positive conclusions. Of particular concern is the fact that very large numbers of school students do not achieve Level 3 or over on PISA literacy tests across the OECD as a whole, raising the question of how well they are equipped with the competences needed for lifetimes of learning in complex knowledge-based societies. The chapter has highlighted a number of other factors that weaken the contribution that schools are making to lifelong learning. The school sector as a whole is still characterised by very low activity and spending on research and development, and by weakly developed networking and knowledge sharing among teaching staff, and the potential of ICT to contribute to better teaching and learning is poorly exploited, as is the potential of career guidance to improve students' progress through complex learning pathways. In addition, teaching and assessment approaches that foster active learning for all students are only patchy in practice, and participation by teachers in professional development varies very widely and is low in some countries. Teachers' careers tend to be too undifferentiated to permit a continuum of professional learning. Finally, the extension of initial education systems has continued apace, in terms of the duration of studies for those with high attainments as well as bringing those with low attainments up to the key thresholds reached by the majority, raising questions about desirability, sustainability, and compatibility with the promotion of lifelong learning.

Working towards lifelong learning through the education provided in schools does not necessarily require whole new batteries of items to add to over-loaded current reform agendas. Rather it demands a scaling up of a range of emergent practices and innovations and greater awareness that the guiding aim of lifelong learning applies as much to schools as it does to all other settings of education and training. Indeed, the broader perspective of moving towards lifelong learning can bring a strategic perspective to school reform rather than reform sticking closely to the achievements and targets that systems have set themselves. In the language of the OECD scenarios, it means more systematic movement towards the models of "re-schooling", possibly combined with some "de-schooling" for older school students, away from the rigidities of the bureaucratic status quo.

References

Artelt, C., J. Baumert, N. Julius McElvany and J. Peschar (2003), *Learners for Life: Student Approaches to Learning, Results from PISA 2000*, OECD, Paris.

Black, P. and D. Wiliam (1998), *Inside the Black Box: Raising Standards through Classroom Assessment*, School of Education, King's College, London, and *Phi Delta Kappan*, Vol. 80(2), pp. 139-148.

Bryce, J., T. Frigo, P. McKenzie and G. Withers (2000), *The Era of Lifelong Learning: Implications for Secondary Schools*, Australian Council for Educational Research, Camberwell Victoria.

Carnoy, M. (2002), "ICT in Education: Possibilities and Challenges", Discussion Paper for the OECD/Japan Seminar "The Effectiveness of ICT in Schools: Current Trends and Future Prospects", Tokyo, 5-6 December.

Duval, R. (2003), "The Retirement Effects of Old-Age Pension and Early Retirement Schemes in OECD Countries", OECD Economics Department Working Papers, No. 370, OECD, Paris.

Istance, D. (2003), "Schooling and Lifelong Learning: Insights from OECD Analyses", *European Journal of Education*, Vol. 38(1), pp. 85-98.

OECD (1973), *Recurrent Education: A Strategy for Lifelong Learning*, OECD, Paris.

OECD (1996), *Lifelong Learning for All*, OECD, Paris.

OECD (1999), *Combating Exclusion through Adult Learning*, What Works in Innovation in Education Series, OECD, Paris.

OECD (2000a), *Motivating Students for Lifelong Learning*, What Works in Innovation in Education Series, OECD, Paris.

OECD (2000b), *Knowledge Management in the Learning Society*, OECD, Paris.

OECD (2000c), *From Initial Education to Working Life: Making Transitions Work*, OECD, Paris.

OECD (2000d), *Literacy in the Information Age: Final Report of the International Adult Literacy Survey*, OECD, Paris.

OECD (2001a), *Education Policy Analysis, 2001 Edition*, OECD, Paris.

OECD (2001b), *Knowledge and Skills for Life: First Results from PISA 2000*, OECD, Paris.

OECD (2001c), *Learning to Change – ICT in Schools*, Schooling for Tomorrow Series, OECD, Paris.

OECD (2001d), *What Schools for the Future?*, Schooling for Tomorrow Series, OECD, Paris.

OECD (2002), *Education at a Glance – OECD Indicators 2002 Edition*, OECD, Paris.

OECD (2003a), *Networks of Innovation: Towards New Models for Managing Schools and Systems*, Schooling for Tomorrow Series, OECD, Paris.

OECD (2003b), *New Challenges for Educational Research*, Knowledge Management Series, OECD, Paris.

OECD (2003c), *Education Policy Analysis 2003 Edition*, OECD, Paris.

OECD (2003d), *Student Engagement at School – A Sense of Belonging and Participation*, OECD, Paris.

OECD (2003e), *Beyond Rhetoric: Adult Learning Policies and Practices*, OECD, Paris.

OECD (2004a), *Innovation in the Knowledge Economy: Implications for Education and Learning*, Knowledge Management Series, OECD, Paris.

OECD (2004b), *Completing the Foundation for Lifelong Learning: An OECD Survey of Upper Secondary Schools*, OECD, Paris.

OECD (2004c), "The Quality of the Teaching Workforce", *OECD Policy Brief*, OECD, Paris, February.

OECD (2004d), *Career Guidance and Public Policy: Bridging the Gap*, OECD, Paris.

OECD (2004e), *Education at a Glance – OECD Indicators 2004 Edition*, OECD, Paris.

OECD (2004f), *Reviews of National Policies for Education – Denmark: Lessons from PISA 2000*, OECD, Paris.

OECD (2004g), "OECD in Figures: Statistics on the Member Countries", *OECD Observer 2003/Supplement 1*, OECD, Paris.

OECD (2005a), *Teachers Matter: Attracting, Developing and Retaining Effective Teachers*, OECD, Paris.

OECD (2005b), *Formative Assessment – Improving Learning in Secondary Classrooms*, OECD, Paris.

Rychen, D.S. and L.H. Salganik (eds.) (2003), *Key Competences for a Successful Life and a Well-Functioning Society*, Hogrefe & Huber, Göttingen.

Schuller, T., H.G. Schuetze and D. Istance (2002), "From Recurrent Education to the Knowledge Society: An Introduction", in D. Istance, H.G. Schuetze and T. Schuller (eds.), *International Perspectives on Lifelong Learning: From Recurrent Education to the Knowledge Society*, The Society for Research into Higher Education and Open University Press, Buckingham (pp.1-21).

Data for Figure 3.1

15-year-olds reaching specified thresholds on PISA combined reading literacy scale, 2000 (%)

	Level 3 and above	Level 1 or below
Mexico	26	44
Luxembourg	37	35
Portugal	48	26
Greece	50	24
Belgium (Fr.)	52	28
Hungary	52	23
Poland	53	23
Germany	55	23
Italy	56	19
Czech Republic	58	18
Spain	58	16
Switzerland	58	20
Denmark	60	18
United States	61	18
France	63	15
Norway	63	18
Iceland	64	15
Austria	64	15
Sweden	67	13
United Kingdom	68	13
Australia	69	12
New Zealand	69	14
Ireland	71	11
Japan	72	10
Canada	72	10
Belgium (Fl.)	74	12
Korea	76	6
Finland	79	7

Source: OECD (2001b, Table 2.1a).

Data for Figure 3.3

Students with a low sense of belonging at school, 2000 (%)

	%
Korea	41
Poland	41
Japan	38
Belgium (Fl.)	32
Belgium (Fr.)	31
France	30
Czech Republic	30
Luxembourg	28
United States	25
Spain	24
Italy	23
Greece	23
Germany	23
Iceland	22
Mexico	22
Finland	21
Norway	21
New Zealand	21
Denmark	21
Switzerland	21
Australia	21
Portugal	21
Canada	21
Austria	20
Ireland	19
Hungary	19
Sweden	18
United Kingdom	17

Source: OECD (2003d).

Data for Figure 3.4

Upper secondary teachers who participated in professional development activities in the 2000-01 school year, according to principals (%)

	Professional development activities excluding ICT-related	ICT-related professional development activities
Hungary	30	19
France	32	20
Korea	33	35
Italy	36	23
Portugal	37	26
Ireland	40	28
Spain	40	29
Mexico	46	31
Belgium (Fl.)	48	30
Country mean	48	32
Norway	56	44
Switzerland	56	28
Netherlands[1]	57	45
Denmark	66	52
Finland	69	43
Sweden	84	37

1. Country did not meet international sampling requirements.
Source: OECD (2004b, Table 3.12).

Data for Figure 3.5

Expected years in education and not in education for 15-to-29-year-olds, 2002

	In education	Employed	Unemployed or not in the labour market	Total
Finland	8.1	4.2	2.7	6.9
Denmark	8.1	6.0	0.9	6.9
France	8.0	5.2	1.8	7.0
Iceland	8.0	6.2	0.8	7.0
Poland	7.9	3.9	3.1	7.1
Sweden	7.5	6.4	1.2	7.5
Germany	7.3	5.9	1.8	7.7
Luxembourg	6.9	6.9	1.1	8.1
Norway	6.8	7.1	1.1	8.2
Canada	6.8	6.4	1.9	8.2
Switzerland	6.7	6.9	1.4	8.3
Australia	6.7	6.4	1.9	8.3
United States	6.6	6.4	2.0	8.4
Belgium	6.5	6.4	2.1	8.5
Hungary	6.4	5.7	2.9	8.6
OECD mean	6.4	6.4	2.2	8.6
Spain	6.3	6.5	2.3	8.7
Italy	6.2	5.7	3.1	8.8
Greece	6.1	6.1	2.8	8.9
United Kingdom	6.0	7.1	1.9	9.0
Austria	5.9	7.5	1.5	9.1
Netherlands	5.9	7.8	1.3	9.1
Ireland	5.7	7.8	1.5	9.3
Portugal	5.6	7.9	1.5	9.4
Czech Republic	5.2	7.3	2.5	9.8
Slovak Republic	5.2	5.8	4.0	9.8
Mexico	4.4	7.0	3.6	10.6
Turkey	3.2	5.9	5.9	11.8

Source: OECD (2004e, Table C4.1a).

HOW WELL DO SCHOOLS CONTRIBUTE
TO LIFELONG LEARNING?

Data for Figure 3.6

Expected years in education before age 30 of 15-year-olds (2002) and percentage of time in education expected to be combined with employment

	Total expected years in education	Percentage of time in education expected to be combined with employment
Switzerland	6.7	58
Denmark	8.1	57
Netherlands	5.9	53
Australia	6.7	53
Iceland	8.0	49
United Kingdom	6.0	42
Canada	6.8	41
United States	6.6	40
Germany	7.3	35
Norway	6.8	32
Finland	8.1	32
Austria	5.9	28
OECD mean	6.4	27
Sweden	7.5	22
Czech Republic	5.2	19
Mexico	4.4	17
Slovak Republic	5.2	17
France	8.0	15
Poland	7.9	14
Ireland	5.7	14
Portugal	5.6	11
Spain	6.2	10
Hungary	6.4	9
Turkey	3.2	9
Luxembourg	6.9	8
Belgium	6.5	7
Greece	6.1	5
Italy	6.2	4

Source: OECD (2004e, Table C4.1a).

Chapter 4

TAXATION AND LIFELONG LEARNING

SUMMARY

Tax policy is one way that governments can support adult investment in learning, reflecting the social as well as individual benefits that such investment brings. Although tax policy is in practice used in many ways to support lifelong learning, this is often done accidentally and unevenly, rather than as part of a consistent strategy.

Tax concessions may apply to revenues earned from selling learning services, or to expenditure on learning by individuals or companies. In both cases they can potentially distort investment in human capital. People and organisations may benefit unevenly according to their income level and their marginal rate of tax. The actual effect of current policies is unknown. Educational and financial authorities need to collaborate more closely to take stock of current policy and its impact, and to consider the need for more consistent approaches.

1. INTRODUCTION

Lifelong learning is integral to strategies for facilitating the transition to a knowledge society, and ensuring that the social and economic benefits of such a society are equitably distributed. However, the ways in which lifelong learning occurs and is paid for – the "institutional arrangements" to support lifelong learning – are far from developed, particularly for adults. The timing, duration, and cost of adult learning, as well as the distribution of its benefits, are different from those that apply to systems of initial education and training. Even traditional formal education is under pressure as, for example, expansion of participation in tertiary education depends increasingly on private financing by students and their families. As education and training systems evolve to become more comprehensive systems of lifelong learning, these shortcomings in "institutional arrangements" will challenge the economic and financial sustainability of such systems as well as their social acceptance over the long term.

Earlier work by the OECD has looked at measures taken by governments and social partners in different countries to ensure that investment in lifelong learning is economically and financially sustainable (OECD, 2000; OECD, 2001; OECD, 2002a; OECD, 2002b; OECD, 2003a; OECD, 2003b; OECD, 2003c; OECD, 2003d; OECD, 2004a). This requires enhanced flexibility of existing arrangements, greater coherence across policy areas, and sometimes entirely new institutional arrangements. Policy discussions have placed particularly strong emphasis on *co-financing* of lifelong learning as a key element in these innovations, reflecting the facts that the benefits of lifelong learning are shared among individuals, employers and society at large, and that no one party may have sufficiently strong incentives or adequate financial means to make investments. There is a wide spectrum of means and mechanisms for sharing financial burdens; many have been tried in recent initiatives launched by governments as well as social partners and financial institutions.

Some policy makers and stakeholders draw attention to tax policy as a public policy lever for implementing co-financing strategies. Tax policy can influence both the economic incentive to invest in lifelong learning and the availability of the financial means for such investment, as well as serving as a mechanism for apportioning incentives and financial responsibilities among different actors (OECD, 2004a, pp. 183-224). Moreover, as tax policy has been used to encourage other forms of capital investment, there is a natural question as whether it should be used to facilitate investment in human capital. There is no consensus among policy makers as to whether tax policy should be brought to bear as a tool to influence investment in lifelong learning. However, regardless of whether tax policy *should be brought to bear*, currently it *is part of the policy environment* in which various initiatives to facilitate the financing of lifelong learning operate. The question of interest to public policy makers is whether this "accidental policy" could and should be more deliberate.

The purpose of this chapter is to identify and explore issues related to the potential role of tax policy in the context of strategies to support lifelong learning by recalling some of the relevant principles that guide tax policy generally, examining their implications for lifelong learning, and examining in more detail their application in a few selected countries. The focus is on lifelong learning for adults, but wider implications are identified as well. The chapter first summarises the economic and financial challenges raised by lifelong learning and notes the emerging interest in tax policy as a possible element in such strategies. It then considers the potential influence of tax policy on incentives to invest in lifelong learning, and examines policy in a few selected countries; it concludes by identifying policy and research questions for further consideration.

2. STRATEGIES FOR SUSTAINABLE INVESTMENT IN LIFELONG LEARNING

This chapter argues that implementation of lifelong learning is hobbled by a mismatch between the institutional arrangements designed for traditional formal education and training systems, and the challenges posed by lifelong learning. The mismatches are particularly acute for adults. Remedies need to be far-reaching.

2.1. The economics and finance of lifelong learning for adults

The policy focus on lifelong learning can be characterised as an effort to overcome shortcomings in education systems in meeting the challenges of the knowledge society. By the mid-1990s it was evident that, though formal education systems were largely keeping up with the demand for *initial* education, they were not able to meet all the learning demands of the knowledge society. In view of the importance of early development for subsequent learning, there was an evident need to strengthen arrangements for early childhood education and care. It was also apparent that adults with low levels of initial qualifications were not only facing increasing difficulty in finding and holding employment, but they were having difficulty in gaining effective access to opportunities for upgrading and updating their knowledge and know-how (OECD/US Department of Education, 1999; OECD, 2003a). By the beginning of the current decade most member countries had made substantial progress in improving learning opportunities for young children (OECD, 2002a). But OECD education ministers noted in 2001 that the lifelong learning agenda still had much to accomplish, particularly with regard to adults.

There are multiple barriers to achieving the goal of making lifelong learning a reality for all adults. Recent analysis by the OECD underlines the importance of appropriate pedagogy, flexibility in the organisation of formal studies, adequate recognition of skills and competences acquired outside formal education and training settings, and support for individuals to allow them better to balance the demands of work, family *and* learning (OECD, 2003a). Progress in these areas is necessary, but is not a sufficient condition for making lifelong learning a reality for all.

Economic and financial barriers are among the most important obstacles to individual participation in lifelong learning and to ensuring adequate overall levels of investment in lifelong learning. Constraints on time typically are cited as the biggest barrier to learning (OECD, 2003a).[1] These "time constraints" are really economic constraints in the form of the prohibitive cost of foregoing earnings during time off from work (or the unwillingness of employers to grant paid leave because of the cost of foregone production) and/or competing claims on non-work time owing to family responsibilities and other priorities. For many, direct costs may be less important because often employers cover part or all of the fees for education and training opportunities; often adult enrolments in formal institutions are at no direct cost to participants.[2] Financial constraints arise because of the presence of "externalities" – the fact that the benefits of adult learning are spread so widely among individuals, employers and the state. This means that even where there is a sufficient overall economic return, no single actor has the incentive to make the whole investment. Thus, unless the financial sharing of costs of adult lifelong learning corresponds to the flow of benefits, there is a heightened risk of under-investment. Financial constraints also are linked to the investment nature of lifelong learning requiring current expenditure that is funded out of past or future earnings.

The contrast with *initial* education and training[3] is striking (see Table 4.1). There, publicly financed systems address the problems of externalities and the timing of financing; the substantial social

---

1. Such constraints may be exacerbated by institutional rigidities – the absence of modular courses or evening classes. But even with more flexible learning opportunities, claims on time for work and/or family responsibilities often crowd out opportunities for participating in education and training.

2. However, direct costs can be an issue to some groups, *e.g.* those seeking to return to the workforce, those seeking to change career in a direction not supported by their current career, self-employed and employees of small businesses, retired persons and persons acquiring skills for unpaid or voluntary work.

3. Initial education and training refers here to education and training that takes place in a formal setting and precedes entry into full-time employment.

returns are symmetrical with the shared burden of financing that is accomplished through tax systems. Such systems also make it possible to finance current education and training expenditure with taxes levied on earnings of earlier beneficiaries of education and training as well as other sources (*e.g.* consumption and property taxes). Such systems address the problem of the mismatch between the timing of cost (incurred during education and training) and the timing of benefits, by relying on taxes to finance on a "pay as you go basis", debt instruments (use of loans and bonds) to finance out of future earnings, and in some countries, incentives to encourage savings for education purposes.

Table 4.1 Economic and financial constraints on investment in learning		
Constraints	**Initial education and training**	**Lifelong learning for adults**
Level and distribution of benefits	Substantial social returns benefiting all of society	Some social returns, substantial private returns to individuals and employers
Under-investment due to externalities (asymmetry between flow of benefits and financing burden)	Minimal because of dominant role of public systems financed through broadly levied taxes	Greater because of absence of co-financing mechanisms that can allocate financing burden according to benefits
Capacity to finance current investment through past or future earnings	Public financing on a "pay as you go" basis permits paying for current expenditure through general taxes; use of public debt instruments to pay infrastructure costs through future earnings	Largely private financing on a "pay as you go" basis (in the absence of loan facilities, bonding arrangements)
Risk of low returns to investment	Public financing spreads risk; income contingent repayment loans shift some risk from individuals to government	Employers and individuals assume risk; few instruments for spreading risk

2.2. Interest in a more deliberate role for tax policy in lifelong learning

In various meetings over the past several years OECD ministers for education, labour and finance, senior officials and social partners have endorsed the goals of lifelong learning and the development of strategies to pursue those goals. Foremost among those was the commitment to address the resource issues to ensure that lifelong learning is affordable.[4]

The October 2003 conference, "A systemic approach to co-financing lifelong learning", and supporting work by the OECD examined the experience with mechanisms that permitted sharing among multiple parties of financial burdens of lifelong learning to mirror the sharing of the benefits.

---

4. A high level meeting was held in Ottawa, Canada in December 2000 to address the question of how to raise the benefits of lifelong learning and reduce its costs, thereby strengthening the economic incentives to invest in lifelong learning; a second high level meeting involving ministers was held in Bonn, Germany in October 2003 to address the question of how co-financing mechanisms might be structured to ensure efficient and equitable financing of lifelong learning, and how approaches based on co-financing could be put on a more systemic basis. (For further information see OECD, 2001; OECD, 2004a).

Table 4.2 Overview of schemes for co-financing lifelong learning		
Objectives	**Instruments**	**Initiatives (countries)**
Finance direct costs of learning (fees, books, transportation)	Individual Learning Accounts – contributions by individuals are matched by contributions by government, non-governmental organisations	Individual Learning Accounts (Austria); Individual Learning and Development Account (Belgium – Flanders); Learn $ave (Canada); Learning Accounts – Ikastxekin, Txekinbide, EMAWEB (Basque Region, Spain); Experiment with Learning Accounts (Netherlands); Individual Learning Accounts – Wales (United Kingdom); Individual Development Accounts (United States)
	Loans – Subsidised loans to individuals	Loan Support for Students of Private Technical Institutions (Korea); Career Development Loans (United Kingdom)
	Vouchers/subsidies – provided by public authorities to individuals or employers	Learning Voucher of the Chamber of Labour of Vienna (Austria); Training Voucher Scheme for Employers (Belgium); Training Voucher Scheme for Employees (Belgium – Walloon); Training and Coaching Voucher Schemes for Employees (Belgium – Flanders); Training Cheque (France); Cheque FORCE (France); Micro-computer Cheque (France); Language Cheques (France); Training-Employment Cheque (France); Voucher Courses (Italy); Vocational Ability Development Programme (Korea); Annual Training Cheque (Switzerland); Individual Training Accounts (United States)
	Tax policy – tax deductions, tax credits, and tax-sheltered savings for learning-related expenditure	Deduction of work-related learning expenses from taxable earnings (Australia, Austria, Netherlands); tax allowance for training/training credit (Austria, Netherlands); Lifelong Learning Plan (Canada); Registered Education Savings Plan, Canadian Education Savings Grant (Canada)

Objectives	Instruments	Initiatives (countries)
Table 4.2 (*continued*) **Overview of schemes for co-financing lifelong learning**		
Replace foregone earnings	Direct Income Support – direct payment by government to help support cost of living to education and training	Adult Education Initiative (Sweden); Adult Education Recruitment Grants (Sweden); Adult Learning Grant (United Kingdom)
	Individual Learning Accounts – contributions by individuals from before-tax income, matched by employer	Competence Accounts-Skandia (Sweden)
	Loans – to cover costs of foregone earnings	Career Development Loans (United Kingdom)
	Collective agreements – individuals accept paid education leave in lieu of salary compensation for a portion of overtime	Deutsche Shell AG collective agreement (Germany); Fraport Q-Card (Germany)
Spread risk	Income-contingent repayment loans – individual liability for fees is postponed until graduation, and then paid back as a fixed proportion of income when/if earnings reach a certain pre-determined level	Higher Education Contribution Scheme (Australia); Post-graduate Education Loan Scheme (Australia)

Source: OECD (2004a), pp. 38-39 and input from national authorities.

The co-financing mechanisms considered three broad purposes: to cover direct costs (tuition fees, books, supplies); to pay towards indirect costs (foregone earnings and production); and to share risk associated with investment in lifelong learning. Table 4.2 summarises a wide range of mechanisms actually used to achieve these objectives. They include private individual learning accounts featuring contributions from employers and employees; publicly subsidised loan schemes; joint public/individual learning accounts; and collective agreements between social partners to compensate a share of overtime through provision of paid leave for training.

Tax policy was embedded – deliberately or not – in many of the co-financing schemes that came under consideration in Bonn. For this reason the Chair, Edelgard Bulmahn, the Federal Minister of Education and Research, called on ministries of finance "… to address the issues related to the tax treatment of costs and revenues related to learning activities, relative to other forms of investment and income" (OECD, 2004a, pp. 82-83.). In discussing how to achieve further progress towards genuinely systemic approaches to co-financing lifelong learning, participants made repeated reference to the need for a "whole of government approach" to coordinate different policies found in different ministries. Indeed, in the Conclusions of the Chair, Mrs. Bulmahn argued that "[e]ducation ministries alone cannot build such systems. But they can take the initiative on behalf of learners in building systems for co-financing".

This call for a more systematic integration of tax policy into strategies for co-financing lifelong learning reflected the perception that the *ad hoc* fashion with which tax policy was already being brought to bear heightened the risk of inconsistent and contradictory incentives for investing in lifelong learning. The next section discusses the potential role of tax policy as a tool for influencing such incentives.

3. WHY MIGHT TAX POLICY MATTER FOR LIFELONG LEARNING?

Tax policy has been incorporated into recent initiatives to enhance incentives and means for financing lifelong learning, as well as financing schemes that were launched well before the current debate on lifelong learning got underway. Before considering that experience it is useful to first review some of the general principles that guide tax policy and their possible implications for lifelong learning.

3.1. Context first: general principles guiding tax policy[5]

Governments need to raise money for public spending programmes. That share of costs which is not financed through fees paid directly by users is ultimately financed through taxation. However, because taxation impacts on economic activity the level of taxation and the design of policies for levying taxes need to be considered carefully. In considering the use of tax policy as a tool for achieving wider policy goals there are three issues of overriding importance: consequences for efficiency; consequences for equity; and workability (ease of administration and enforcement).

Insofar as public policy serves narrow efficiency objectives alone, specific taxes should, as a starting point, aim for "neutrality", meaning that they should not distort economic behaviour by steering investment or consumption choices in one particular direction or another. Ideally this implies meeting at least two conditions:

- Achieving a tax base that is as broad as possible (*e.g.* taxing all factors inputs, such as capital and labour, rather than just one factor input; taxing all sources of income rather than just one), with exemptions at a minimum.

- Having as flat a structure of tax rates as possible (*e.g.* taxing the entire wage bill, rather than just the amount above a certain threshold; taxing corporate and individual income at the same rate; taxing all income at the same rate, rather than raising rates at higher income levels).

However the ideal is rarely achieved where governments, as a matter of policy choice, use tax policy to achieve multiple objectives. Even where governments assign first priority to efficiency, "neutrality" may be displaced by other considerations. Governments may find it possible to impose higher taxes on goods and services (such as energy) for which demand is not particularly sensitive to price and substitution is not feasible. Governments may also use tax policy to compensate for market failure, particularly when markets fail to account for "externalities". This may occur for example where prices fail to capture the cost of pollution, leading to excessive use of polluting fuels, or where fears of poaching discourage employers from investing in training.

Moreover, because governments seek to act in the public good, efficiency is not the only objective they pursue: equity matters as well. While efficiency concerns the issue of whether taxes distort economic choice, equity concerns the issue of whether taxes allocate income and wealth fairly. There are two aspects of equity that are relevant: horizontal and vertical equity. Horizontal equity is analogous to the notion of "neutrality". It can be evaluated in terms of whether persons in similar economic conditions pay the same amount of tax. What constitutes "similar economic conditions" is not entirely straightforward and objective. For example, incomes tax systems frequently do not look just at earnings; they also take into account, for example, marital status

---

5. This section draws heavily on van den Noord and Heady (2001); for further background see also: OECD Directorate for Science, Technology and Industry (2002); Immervoll (2004).

and the number of dependents. In this sense the notion of horizontal equity is subjective. If the criteria for defining "similar economic conditions" are too prescriptive they could conceivably weaken neutrality. Vertical equity, the extent to which persons with higher income pay more taxes, is the key measure of the re-distributional impact of tax systems. It typically is evaluated in terms of how much marginal tax rates rise with income.[6] By this measure income tax systems in most countries are progressive; though the extent varies widely (an exception is the Slovak Republic that recently introduced a flat rate tax of 19% that applies to personal and corporate income, as well as to consumption). The progressivity of income tax regimes often is diminished, however, because of unequal distributions of deductions from taxable income and forms of income that are not counted as taxable income.

A last principle guiding tax policy is its practicality – the extent to which it is transparent, easy to administer and enforce, and to which compliance and enforcement are cost-effective. Tax measures that are not practical to administer and enforce (from the point of view of tax authorities), and to comply with (from the point of view of tax payers) invite uneven application and ultimately risk undermining their efficiency (including neutrality) and equity objectives. Conversely, practicality is enhanced insofar as tax measures do not distort choices excessively and are seen as being fair.

The following section considers the specific issue of tax treatment of learning-related expenditure and earnings in view of the principles reviewed above.

3.2. Two channels through which tax policy may influence investment in lifelong learning

There are two main channels through which tax policy may influence investment in lifelong learning: through the tax treatment of revenues from the sale of learning services, and through the tax treatment of expenditure on investment in learning.[7]

Revenues

The first concerns the tax treatment of revenues that education and training providers receive from those who pay for learning services (whether individual learners or their sponsors such as employers or government). This treatment takes the form of taxes on value-added and/or sales as well as taxes on profits. These, like other taxes, impose a "wedge" between what the purchasers of learning-related services pay, and what the providers of such services effectively receive as income. In highly competitive markets (such as computer or language training) where learners have choice among many alternative providers of education and training, providers are under pressure to pass on to learners a relatively small share of the extra cost imposed by taxes. Where there are few alternative providers (and learners have less choice), providers can pass along to learners a larger share of the extra cost imposed by such taxes.

---

6. One indicator of income tax progressivity compares the tax burden of a worker with the average production wage (APW), with that of a worker earning 0.67 APW, to calculate low-wage progressivity; and compares the burden of the former with that of a worker paid 1.67 apw. For further description of calculations for single workers in 1998 see van den Noord and Heady (2001).

7. It could be argued that a third channel is the tax treatment of returns to investment in lifelong learning, and that progressive tax systems act to reduce the incentives for individuals to invest in human capital by raising disproportionately the tax on subsequent increases in earnings. That is not treated here because current policy in most OECD member countries assigns a high priority to preserving progressivity, *i.e.* increasing marginal tax rates with income.

In the context of considering how tax policy affects investment in lifelong learning two questions arise. One is whether the level of taxation on revenues generated by sales of learning activities is comparable to the level of taxation on revenues generated by sales of other forms of investment (*i.e.* do such taxes violate the objective of neutrality). The second is whether all providers of learning services are treated equally, that is, are subject to the same taxes, face similar cost pressures, and are under similar pressures to pass on and absorb the costs imposed by taxes.

Investment in human capital is unlike other forms of investment. From the time that schooling was made compulsory, public sector providers have dominated education and training. Education – at least through the upper secondary level – has been treated as a public good because of the scale of investment involved and because of the substantial social returns that universal education generates. At the level of tertiary education there has been a pattern in some countries of relying on private sources to pay a share of the total financial burden. As tertiary participation has expanded, that private share has grown, and in countries that have been previously entirely publicly funded, there is a trend to support at least part of the expansion through private financing. In the primary, secondary and tertiary sectors there have emerged private sector institutions as well. But because of the long and strong tradition of the public-good nature of education, the issue of tax treatment of revenues has not been an issue. Private institutions are typically tax-exempt because of their not-for-profit status; because of the public-good nature of even privately-provided education such institutions are eligible for public support in many countries.

But lifelong learning – particularly lifelong learning for adults – breaks the mould and generates different challenges. First, because of the evidence of substantial private returns to employers and individuals (OECD, 2004b), lifelong learning for adults is to a lesser extent a "public good" than is schooling, for example, which generates a longer stream of social returns and less direct and immediate private returns than many forms of adult learning. Second, insofar as lifelong learning for adults serves to update and upgrade the competences of adults in response to volatility in workplace qualifications requirements, education and training providers need to be able to respond quickly and to offer more flexible forms of learning. Thus, a key issue is how to make education and training providers more adaptable and able to respond to the needs of learners – including the poorly qualified who are not served well by present arrangements.[8] For-profit providers have the incentives to respond appropriately and, through the potential to earn profits, they have access to the financial means to create the infrastructure that is in demand. This would argue in favour of accommodating the increased demand for lifelong learning by ensuring that at least some of the expansion of learning opportunities is through private, for-profit providers.

In this context, the prevailing practice of taxing revenues earned by for-profit providers, but not those earned by public and not-for-profit providers might violate the principle of horizontal equity by which all actors in comparable economic circumstances are treated equally. In so doing, it puts the for-profit providers of lifelong learning at a competitive disadvantage. Their net earnings are less if they charge the same as public and non-profit institutions for comparable offerings; conversely, they have to charge more for the same course if they are to cover all costs. This effectively operates as a barrier to entry of for-profit providers into a sector in which there is increasing demand for flexible learning opportunities. This risks impinging on the supply of new providers or steering such providers or steering new provision towards higher value-added education and training (benefiting more highly-paid workers). A key consideration, however, is whether for-profit

---

8. Whether or not for-profit providers respond to the needs of poorly qualified adults will depend in part on the degree to which mechanisms for (co-) financing lifelong learning are able to give them "market power". See OECD, 2004a (pp. 34-37) for a discussion of strategies for doing this.

providers provide services that are indeed equivalent to those provided by others; this would argue for further examination.

Expenditure

The second channel through which tax policy may influence investment in lifelong learning is through the tax treatment of expenditure on investment in learning by deducting some amount of expenditure from taxable income, or by giving a tax credit against such spending. Both may be subject to thresholds (when expenditure is below a threshold, tax provisions do not apply) and ceilings (when expenditure is above such ceilings, tax provisions do not apply).

There are several forms of expenditure related to learning and human capital investment, and they are not all treated the same within the framework of tax policy. Earlier work by the OECD (OECD, 2000, 2001, 2004a) identified the principal components of cost associated with lifelong learning as direct costs of learning, such as fees for courses and/or assessment of prior learning, books, and transportation, and indirect costs such as foregone earnings or foregone production. Among costs that are more measurable and verifiable, tax systems differ with respect to their treatment. The prevailing practice has been to allow individuals to deduct expenditure from taxable earnings only when they are undertaken in connection with learning activities that are necessary for current employment. Some countries have begun relaxing those restrictions in line with the objectives of lifelong learning to allow expenditure on learning that is relevant to future employment. Notwithstanding the measurement difficulties, the differential treatment of different cost components does threaten the neutrality principle insofar as it establishes stronger incentives for particular kinds of learning. For example though on-the-job training is found to be far more effective than formal classroom training in reaching particular groups of adults, particularly those with low skills, the tax-based incentives clearly favour the latter because costs are more easily measured and verified.

The tax treatment of expenditure differs according to whether it is undertaken by individuals or employers. Generally, tax policy is more uniform and favourable towards employer expenditure. Direct expenditure for learning-related activities incurred by employers generally is deducted from earnings as a cost of doing business. Some countries have used tax policy to provide an extra incentive for human capital investment in order to offer a stronger incentive for this kind expenditure than expenditure on other business costs, such as advertising or heating and lighting. Austria and the Netherlands, for example, have introduced initiatives (discussed in more detail in the next section) to strengthen the incentive to invest in lifelong learning by allowing employers to deduct from earnings the allowable cost plus a premium. Though the tax-linked human capital investment incentives are not very widespread, they are similar in design and objective to the extra incentives that more than half of OECD countries allow for employer expenditure on R&D (OECD Directorate for Science, Technology and Industry, 2002, pp. 26-30).

The comparative strength of incentives for employers and individuals to invest in human capital (*i.e.* the effective impact of such measures on human capital investment cost – absolute level of cost as well as the cost compared to other kinds of investment) is also a function of how heavily (individual) income and (corporate) profits are taxed. The higher the tax rate on taxable income, the greater is the saving when a cost can be deducted from taxable income. Corporate tax rates usually are fixed at a flat rate for all firms, although about half of all OECD central governments have separate, lower schedules for small and medium sized enterprises (SMEs) (see Table 4.3). In contrast, personal income tax schedules in nearly all countries are progressive, with levels of taxation rising with income (see Table 4.4). Considering that i) the tax-linked incentive to invest in lifelong learning is directly related to the tax rate, and ii) that tax rates differ between employers and employees and by income level, the outcomes are bound to be complex.

Table 4.3 Central government corporate taxes, 2001[1]		
	Central government rate[2]	SME rate
Australia	30.0	same
Austria	34.0	same
Belgium[3]	33.99 (33.0)	24.98
Canada	24.1 (23.0)	13.12
Czech Republic	31.0	n.a.
Denmark	30.0	same
Finland	29.0	same
France[4]	35.43	15.45
Germany	27.96 (26.5)	same
Greece	35.0	same
Hungary	18.0	-
Iceland	18.0	same
Ireland	12.5	12.50
Italy	34.0	same
Japan	30.0	22.0
Korea[5]	27.0	15.00
Luxembourg	22.88	20.80
Mexico	34.0	-
Netherlands[6]	34.5	29.00
New Zealand	33.0	same
Norway	28.0	-
Poland	n.a.	same
Portugal	30.0	20.00
Slovak Republic	25.0	same
Spain[7]	35.0	30.00
Sweden	28.0	same
Switzerland[8]	8.5	same
Turkey	33 (30)	same
United Kingdom[9]	30.0	19.00
United States[10]	35.0	15.00

n.a.: data not provided.

1. This table shows "basic" (non-targeted) central corporate income tax rates. Where a progressive (as opposed to flat) rate structure applies, the top marginal rate is shown. Explanatory notes can be found in OECD Tax Database.

2. This column shows the basic central government statutory (flat or top marginal) corporate income tax rate, measured gross of a deduction (if any) for sub-central tax. Where surtax applies, the statutory corporate rate exclusive of surtax is shown in round brackets.

3. Applicable on the first EUR 25 000 of taxable income when taxable income is less than EUR 332 500. The rates are 31.93% (31) up to a taxable income of EUR 90 000, and 35.535% (34) on the remaining taxable income up to EUR 332 500.

4. These are the rates applying to income earned in 2003, to be paid in 2004. Applicable where turnover does not exceed EUR 7.63 million, and on the part of the profit that does not exceed EUR 38 120.

5. Applicable on first W100 million.

6. Applicable on first EUR 22 689 of taxable income.

7. Qualifying small companies are taxed at 30% on first EUR 90 151.82.

8. These figures from adjusted tax rates are calculated by the Swiss Federal tax administration (for the method and examples, see the working paper: "Quels taux effectifs et nominaux d'imposition des sociétés en Suisse pour le calcul des coins fiscaux. Le procédé de la déduction fiscale en Suisse"). Church taxes are included.

9. For companies with tax-adjusted profits below GBP 300 000 the rate is 19%. For very small companies, the starting rate is zero. Rates as of 5 April.

10. Applicable on first USD 50 000.

Source: OECD Tax Database and information from national authorities.

Table 4.4 Marginal personal income tax rates ("all-in") on gross labour income,[1] 2003

	APW	Tax rates for different income levels			
		Income levels expressed as a percentage of APW			
		67%	100%	133%	167%
Australia[2]	51 190	31.5%	31.5%	48.5%	48.5%
Austria	24 438	42.3%	42.6%	49.8%	49.8%
Belgium	31 385	59.3%	54.8%	59.3%	59.3%
Canada	39 888	27.5%	35.0%	31.1%	39.4%
Czech Republic	195 219	25.6%	30.0%	30.0%	34.4%
Denmark	316 205	43.3%	48.8%	62.3%	62.3%
Finland	28 551	39.3%	45.0%	50.7%	50.7%
France	22 475	47.6%	32.8%	35.6%	35.6%
Germany	33 757	51.3%	57.9%	56.5%	63.1%
Greece	11 805	16.0%	16.0%	28.6%	41.2%
Hungary	1 153 440	40.4%	40.4%	68.4%	68.4%
Iceland	2 720 233	37.0%	37.0%	37.0%	42.0%
Ireland	25 951	24.0%	26.0%	48.0%	44.6%
Italy	22 120	37.1%	44.1%	44.1%	55.8%
Japan	4 217 856	18.7%	22.9%	22.9%	32.0%
Korea	24 887 904	10.9%	12.5%	23.4%	23.4%
Luxembourg	31 763	28.2%	37.1%	47.8%	47.8%
Mexico	63 475	8.8%	15.3%	15.3%	26.7%
Netherlands	31 895	46.5%	45.4%	45.4%	52.0%
New Zealand[2]	40 467	21.0%	33.0%	33.0%	39.0%
Norway	305 653	35.8%	35.8%	49.3%	49.3%
Poland	25 868	34.4%	34.4%	34.4%	34.4%
Portugal	8 671	23.0%	25.0%	35.0%	35.0%
Slovak Republic	150 000	21.5%	30.2%	30.2%	30.2%
Spain	17 149	34.0%	28.8%	32.6%	32.6%
Sweden	244 454	35.5%	35.5%	52.0%	51.2%
Switzerland	63 720	23.4%	29.0%	34.2%	34.2%
Turkey	12 635 661 981	32.6%	32.6%	36.9%	36.8%
United Kingdom[2]	19 960	33.0%	33.0%	33.0%	23.0%
United States	33 553	29.1%	29.1%	39.1%	39.1%

APW = average production wage (in national currency), meaning the average annual gross wage earnings of adult, full-time workers in the manufacturing sector.

1. This table reports marginal personal income tax and social security contribution rates for a single person without dependents, at various multiples (67%, 100%, 133%, 167%) of the APW. The results, derived from the OECD Taxing Wages framework (elaborated in the annual publication *Taxing Wages*), use tax rates applicable to the tax year beginning in calendar year 2003. The results take into account basic/standard income tax allowances and tax credits relevant to central and sub-central government taxes plus employee social security contributions.

2. Country in which the tax year is not the calendar year.

Source: OECD Tax Database – Taxation of Wage Income, Table I.1.

It is difficult to judge the treatment of individuals and employers with respect to the principle of "horizontal equity". Though they face very different situations with respect to the tax treatment of their expenditure, their circumstances certainly differ. For one thing, employers will undertake learning-related investment exclusively for purposes related to the running of a company, while individuals may take on such expenditure for a variety of work and non-work related reasons. As for the principle of "vertical equity", the effect of tax policies to allow individuals to deduct learning-related expenditure from taxable income is to invert the re-distributional effects of progressive tax systems. This is discussed further below.

Considerations about ultimate impacts

In considering the ultimate impact of tax policy on investment in human capital there are at least two criteria by which measures need to be judged: the impact on aggregate levels of investment in human capital and the impact on the distribution of opportunities.[9] One direct measure of aggregate impact is the "tax expenditure" associated with a particular measure, the total amount of taxes foregone because of expenditure being deducted from taxable income, tax credits to offset expenditure, tax exemptions, etc. Another related measure is "take-up rates" – the extent to which taxpayers (*e.g.* employers, individuals) respond to the availability of particular measures. But tax expenditure is only a first approximation of the extent to which a given tax measure actually influences behaviour and, for example, stimulates *net new* investment in human capital. Net impacts may be diminished by *deadweight effects* attributable to taxpayers simply substituting public resources (in the form of tax breaks) for the private resources that they would have spent anyway to pay for investment in human capital. Net impacts may be diminished as well by *spill-over effects* – collateral, sometimes under-anticipated impacts that diminish the effectiveness of a policy intervention in question. Box 4.1 reviews the results of an evaluation on an initiative in the Netherlands.

Box 4.1 Assessing the impact of tax policy on human capital investment

In 1998 the authorities in the Netherlands introduced a new initiative that, among other things, allowed employers to deduct 140% of training costs expended on employees 40 years or older. The purpose was to counteract the pattern of declining training rates observed among older workers at a time when training was seen to be increasingly important for their employability and firm competitiveness. One evaluation (Leuven and Oosterbeek, 2000) found that following the introduction of the initiative, training rates of workers just above age 40 were 15-20% higher than rates for comparable workers just below age 40. Thus the initiative appeared to have stimulated a shift in training behaviour. However, further evaluation also found that the volume of training that resulted from this increase among persons over 40 was more than offset by a decline in training rates among the younger workers, leading the authors of the study to concluded that "[t]he estimates of the spill-over effects on workers younger than 40 indicate that these spill-overs are so substantial that the net effect of the age-dependent tax deduction is negative" (Leuven and Oosterbeek, 2000, p. 18). The authors did note that with time (the evaluation was carried out less than two years after the initiative was introduced), as those under age 40 at the time of the evaluation passed the age of 40, their training rates might rise enough to generate overall net positive effects. However, they underlined the importance of taking spill-over effects into account.

---

9. The question of the impact on aggregate economic activity of changes in tax policy regarding human capital investment is beyond the scope of this chapter.

Impact is most readily assessed in the case of the tax treatment of expenditure. Who benefits from favourable tax treatment of expenditure on lifelong learning, and how does this relate to prevailing patterns of participation in lifelong learning? Insofar as tax policies favour investment in lifelong learning by allowing expenditure to be deducted from individuals' taxable income, the effect is greatest in absolute terms for persons with higher income (who are, on average, better qualified to begin with). This is because under progressive tax systems, marginal tax rates rise with income. Table 4.5 illustrates the example of individuals at different income levels undertaking training whose cost is equal to 100% of the average production wage (APW). If all workers spend the same amount of money on training, the savings are greatest in absolute terms for the higher income individuals. They are *proportionately* greater for low income individuals in this example because the savings, though smaller in absolute terms, represent a larger share of earnings of the lower income persons. However, this proportional gain is not likely to be realised insofar as lower income individuals are, on average, less likely to undertake learning-related activities (there is a virtually universal pattern in OECD member countries of a strong, positive relationship between adults' participation in learning and the level of their initial education, which in turn, is strongly related to income).

Furthermore, this overestimates the benefits also because among those individuals at the lower end of the earnings distribution who actually do incur learning-related expenditure, a substantial number do not even pay income tax, and therefore get no benefit from a tax break for such expenditure. Table 4.6 presents aggregate measures of the income threshold at which income taxes begin to apply in the OECD. The thresholds are presented as a percentage of the average production wage (APW). The higher the threshold, the more an individual must earn before being able to benefit from deductions for learning-related expenditure (or for other kinds of expenditure, such as interest paid on a home mortgage). The table shows that in the OECD as a whole, workers from one-earner families with two children, who earn only slightly less than the APW wage pay no income tax (and enjoy no benefit from deducting learning-related expenditure).

Thus tax treatment defined just in terms of deductions from taxable income does nothing to redress the inequities in participation between persons with different educational attainment levels, and, at an aggregate level may (depending on actual spending by level of income) have perverse re-distributional consequences. The effects can be made more equitable through provisions that, for example, set ceilings on deductions for higher income individuals, or allow for tax credits for lower income individuals. But adjustments such as these may increase administrative complexity and compliance cost.

Table 4.5 **Example of benefits of tax deduction for a given training expenditure of USD 1 000, by income level**

Individual earnings	Tax rate[1]	Amount of deduction	After-tax cost	Savings as % of income
High income individual[2]	45%	USD 450	USD 550	–
167% APW[3]	29%	USD 290	USD 710	17%
100% APW[3]	19%	USD 190	USD 810	19%
67% APW[3]	16%	USD 160	USD 840	24%

1. Unweighted average of OECD countries; tax rate corresponds to highest personal tax rate (2000); medium and low income rates correspond to earnings equal to 100% and 67% of the average production wage (2003).
2. With earnings above the threshold at which the maximum marginal tax rate applies.
3. APW = average production wage.

Source: Secretariat calculations and OECD Tax Database.

Table 4.6 Income thresholds at which income tax rates begin to apply

As a percentage of the average production wage (APW), results for 2003

	Single, no children	Single, two children	One-income earner family, no children	One-income earner family, two children
OECD unweighted average (income tax less benefits)	31.0	84.9	43.7	91.4
OECD median value (income tax less benefits)	29.0	80.6	46.6	89.2

Source: OECD (2004c), pp. 42-44.

3.3. Accidental implications of tax policy for lifelong learning?

There are a number of ways in which tax policy can, in principle, facilitate or thwart national policies for lifelong learning through its influence over costs and incentives on both the supply and demand side. What this implies for policy makers responsible for formulating and implementing strategies for lifelong learning is not entirely clear. Tax authorities in many OECD member countries are reluctant to bring tax policy to bear as a tool for achieving outcomes other than raising revenues. Indeed, recent initiatives in a number of countries have gone in the direction of lowering overall tax rates, reducing complexity by reducing the number of tax rates and limiting deductions and tax credits.[10]

But the fact remains that in most countries the systems send mixed signals with respect to investment in lifelong learning – incentives facing different actors vary, and the incentives to invest in lifelong learning compared to other "assets" also vary. What impact they finally have depends on the mix of policies in place; the extent to which they are mutually reinforcing or not; and the forces competing with the effects of tax policy.

The following section examines actual policies that are in place in a few countries. The discussion is intended to illustrate the application of some of the principles and concepts reviewed above, and to identify issues that merit further investigation.

4. THE ROLE OF TAX POLICY IN RECENT INITIATIVES: OVERVIEW OF EXPERIENCE IN THREE COUNTRIES[11]

In recent experimentation with mechanisms to permit the co-financing of lifelong learning, governments have shown particular readiness to rely on tax policy as a co-financing method. Though this has been most obvious in the past few years, tax policy has played a role in financing

---

10. The Slovak Republic has gone so far as to adopt a single flat rate tax (19%) on personal and corporate income and consumption. It would appear that this is part of the leading edge of a trend towards lowering at least corporate tax rates. The trend in overall tax burdens is not so clear as there is evidence that taxes on labour have begun to rise again after falling for several years (OECD Tax Database; OECD, 2004c).

11. This section draws heavily on Jansen (2003). The report was prepared as part of a cooperative effort by the OECD and the European Learning Account Partners Network (ELAP) to document and examine recent developments related to co-financing lifelong learning.

schemes long before that. One of the earliest was the "levy exemption scheme", typified by the oft-copied French law of 1971 that imposes a tax on enterprises equal to a fixed percentage of the payroll (originally set at 1.1% of gross payroll in the case of France, it now is 1.5% of gross payroll), but which is reduced by the amount that enterprises spend on allowable training activities. The rationale behind such "train-or-pay" schemes was to reduce the incentive for employers to lower costs by not training. That approach was copied by a number of other countries. More recently there have been newer initiatives that have relied on tax policy in other ways. The following section examines specific experience in three countries: Austria, Finland and the Netherlands.

4.1. Austria[12]

The Austrian training systems concentrate on initial training. Historically, adult education and continuing vocational training go back to initiatives of professional associations, churches, political parties and trade unions. Over time, a relatively pluralistic continuing education and training (CET) system with public, semi-public and private providers and a great variety of programmes and providers has developed, financed by multiple parties.

Until recently, the conditions under which training expenses were accepted as income-related expenses by the Austrian financial authorities were quite strict. However, under recent legislation these conditions have been relaxed, whilst incentives for companies to spend on training have been strengthened.

Treatment of revenues

Under the Value Added Tax Act (§ 6 Abs. 1 Z 11 und 12 UStG 1994), revenues of private schools and other providers of general or vocational education and training are exempt from VAT (*unechte Umsatzsteuerbefreiung*) if their programmes are comparable to those of public schools. The revenues of not-for-profit corporations under public law and the revenues of other not-for-profit associations offering courses on general or vocational education to a broad public are also exempt. Organisations thus exempted from VAT do not have to charge VAT to their clients. On the other hand, however, they cannot recover the VAT they pay themselves. There is a reduced VAT rate of 10% for books and periodicals.

Treatment of expenditure

For the calculation of income tax, training expenses are treated as income-related expenses reducing taxable income. This is accomplished in the annual income tax assessment. Persons paying wage tax have to claim these expenses in their annual tax return. Until recently, the conditions under which training expenses were accepted as income-related expenses by the financial authorities were quite strict. Only the cost of training measures deemed necessary for the individual to maintain his or her current job or, in the case of self-employed persons, training expenses directly related to their professional field, qualified as income-related expenses.

However, recent amendments to the Income Tax Act (2000 and 2002) introduced a more flexible approach. The current provisions take into consideration all expenses for training related to the individual's professional field, as well as expenses for long-term training measures leading to a

---

12. Based on material submitted by Thomas Mayr and Kurt Schmid, Institute for Research on Qualification and Training of the Austrian Economy (ibw), Vienna.

broad vocational re-qualification (*i.e.* leading to completely new qualifications).[13] Basically, all training measures with some degree of vocational orientation are eligible in this context. Typical examples would be IT courses, business-related courses, language courses, and vocational evening schools (second chance schools). Not deductible are expenses for general and academic education and for training which is primarily intended for private purposes, such as sports courses or training for a regular driver's license. Expenses for a driver's license for a truck are deductible if this license is required for the individual's job. The details of what type of training qualifies as vocational training are set out in the guidelines on the Income Tax Act which are issued regularly by the Ministry of Finance and published on its website. These definitions seem to be workable. According to the Ministry, there have only been a few cases of legal remedies against adverse decisions.

Since 2000, Austrian employers, irrespective of the legal form of their company, can claim an extra tax allowance for training expenses (*Bildungsfreibetrag*). The target group for this measure is formed by all employees of a company irrespective of their position, age, specific training needs, etc. The goal is to promote companies' investment in human resources. This training incentive is regulated by the Income Tax Act (§4 Abs 4 ESTG 1988) and has the form of an extra deduction from taxable profits. This means that not only the actual expense for training is deducted from taxable income, but also an extra "virtual expense".

When the measure was introduced in 2000, the tax allowance was 9% of expenses for external training (*e.g.* courses offered by training providers not belonging to the company itself). In 2002, the tax allowance was increased to 20% and extended to in-company training. This incentive allows companies to deduct an extra 20% of the actual training expense from their taxable profits. This leads to a reduction of the tax base by 120% of the actual expense, which in turn leads to a lower tax liability.

Companies that do not make enough profit to benefit from the 120% tax allowance can alternatively claim a tax credit of 6% of the actual expense (*Bildungsprämie*). The training credit is subject to the same criteria as the tax allowance. Employers can only receive the training credit if they have not already claimed the tax allowance. The training credit has to be claimed in the framework of the employer's tax return and is deducted from tax liability; it qualifies therefore as a direct tax credit.

Recent discussions on tax treatment

So far no comprehensive evaluation of the special tax measures relating to training expenses has been conducted. However, for political reasons decisions were taken to soften the criteria for

---

13. The following training expenses are accepted by the financial authorities as income-related expenses: course fees, expenses for books, travelling costs, daily expenses including hotel costs for the first five days, if the course is not held in the place of residence or at the work place. In order for companies to claim the extra tax allowance (deduction of 120% of the actual costs) for training their employees, the training activities must meet the following criteria: the training must be provided by a training organisation different and independent from the company claiming the tax allowance; the recipients of the training must be employees of the company; the training has to be in the company's interest and has to be fully paid for by the employer claiming the tax allowance; there is no upper ceiling for the claim of the extra tax allowance.

For companies, in order to claim the extra allowance for internal training, the following criteria have to be met: expenses have to result from training measures the company organised for and offered to its employees; a certain independence and organisational autonomy of the training department or body is necessary (*e.g.* a company academy or a subsidiary); the training measure must be a formal training (*e.g.* a course, a seminar) and must be verifiable (*e.g.* proof of attendance lists, invitation, curricula, etc.). The maximum expense per day for the tax allowance is EUR 2 000, irrespective of the number of participants. Expenses for which the extra allowance can be claimed: course fees; fees for speakers and trainers; expenses for books and other learning materials; rent for rooms (outside the company) and training equipment needed (*e.g.* audio-visual equipment).

These criteria are defined in the Income Tax Act and – in more detail – in the guidelines on the Income Tax Act.

training expenses to count as "income-related expenses" and to increase the extra tax allowance for companies from 9% to 20%. These measures were welcomed by the social partners and the training sector. They are regarded as providing a clear incentive for investment in training, without creating a huge bureaucratic and administrative burden.

A current draw-back of the extra tax allowance might be that it is not yet well known. However, as training providers have begun to print information about this special tax treatment of training expenses prominently on the first pages of their brochures, more people and especially those in personnel departments, become aware of these measures. For Austria's employers' organisation, the Austrian Economic Chamber, the extra tax allowance is an important instrument acknowledging the importance of firm-based training in an overall lifelong learning strategy. As the measure is seen to have an important steering effect, the Economic Chamber proposes to increase the rate to 40% for small enterprises and certain target groups (such as older workers, low qualified workers, people returning to work after child leave, etc.).

4.2. Finland[14]

Since the 1990s Finland has been one of the fastest growing economies in Europe thanks in part to the establishment in 1985 of Science and Technology Policy Council to formulate and monitor innovation strategy. As part of the innovation process, the Ministries of Education and Finance formed a new taskforce for the co-financing of lifelong learning. Finland has used policy coordination to develop an effective lifelong learning system. Except for basic university education, adults can participate in all levels of certificate-oriented and non-certificate-oriented education organised specifically for them. Adults are given opportunities to complete primary or general upper secondary education by means of distance education. Fifty eight per cent of Finnish adults aged 25-64 participated in learning within the 12 months prior to an adult literacy survey conducted in 1998.

Treatment of revenues

Educational services provided in accordance with the law or subsidised from State funds in accordance with statutory provisions are exempt from VAT. The following entities (amongst others) are exempt from income tax (Taxation in Finland 2001): the University of Helsinki, the Regional development fund, the Nordic development fund, employee investment funds, sports training funds, the Finnish National Fund for Research and Development. Not-for-profit organisations in the field of education, science and arts, etc., have to pay corporate income tax only on their business profits. No gift tax is levied on household effects received as gifts and intended for the beneficiary's (or his family's) education or maintenance.

Treatment of expenditure

The main principle underlying Finnish taxation is that costs incurred in earning income and maintaining professional/vocational skills are deductible from taxable income. Training that develops and maintains existing professional/vocational competences is a non-taxable benefit. On the other hand, employer-financed training that clearly raises the professional/vocational competence level and prepares for new duties has been considered a benefit comparable to pay and therefore treated as taxable income. Nor is the expenditure deductible when the employee finances this kind of training him-/herself. For the employer the cost of any staff development training is tax-deductible.

---

14. This sub-section is based on material submitted by Merja Leinonen, Ministry of Education, Finland.

In general, expenses are deductible if they are incurred for the purpose of acquiring or maintaining income. For employees there is a standard deduction (EUR 590 in 2003) for work-related expenses from earned income. There are no tax regulations concerning expenses for training provided by the employer, nor for work-related training expenses paid by the employee. For the employee, "own expenses", i.e. those not paid by the employer, related to primary education and further education resulting in a degree, are usually (with a few exceptions) not considered to be deductible from an individual's taxable income. The same applies to such courses when they are paid by the employer.

For the employee, training/education provided by the employer is usually considered tax-free from a legal perspective, if it is regarded as a necessity for maintaining and/or developing the required professional skills for the current tasks, and the employee has had a basic training/education for these tasks. In this case, if the training is necessary from the employer's perspective, education resulting in a degree can also be regarded as tax-free income for the employee. If the training is not considered to be tax-free, it is considered as wages and taxed as earned income. For example MBA degrees paid for by the employer are quite often tax-free, if they meet the criteria for tax-free education (i.e. necessary for maintaining employment).

Generally, training expenses are deductible for the employer when the benefit is tax-free for the employee receiving the training.

In practice, it has proved difficult to draw a clear line between the two kinds of education/training. The decisions have been made case by case. The same kind of training may have been treated differently for tax purposes, depending on participants' educational backgrounds and the nature of their jobs. This has been a particular problem in the assessment of highly educated people's education/training costs, which may be considerable.

Special attention has been paid to MBA programmes. If the education is considered a benefit comparable to pay, it has repercussions for the recipient in taxation. This is exacerbated by the fact that no tax is deducted from pay in advance because it is looked upon as a benefit in kind. Attention has also been paid to the fact that participation in this kind of education does not necessarily yield any immediate taxable benefit to the participant.

Recent discussions on tax treatment of post-initial training

The harmonisation of taxation in the EU member states will put pressure on Finland to lower the tax rate, which may result in lower tax income and thereby restrict leeway in public finance.[15]

In March 2001 the Ministry of Education appointed an adult education committee, which had as one task to put forward proposals concerning the resources required by the new policy lines, the allocation of the resources and the financing base. In its report the committee proposed that measures be taken without delay to clarify the taxation of longer term in-service training and to remove any obstacles to education/training due to taxation. Consequently, the Ministry of Education appointed a one-man commission to look into this matter and propose measures needed to clarify the taxation of longer-term training paid by the employer. In November 2003 the committee submitted its report on measures geared to improve conditions for adult education in Finland.

The report proposed two measures concerning taxation. First, to revise the Finnish Tax Administration guidelines concerning training expenses to guide tax offices to treat training expenses as allowable

---

15. Ministry of Education, Strategy 2015 (2003), Helsinki.

expenses entitling to tax deduction. Secondly, to use more widely precedents concerning the treatment of training costs in taxation. Based on the report and comments received subsequently, the Ministry of Education drew up a plan for preparation of further measures. According to it, the ministries will assume the main responsibility for implementing the proposals in their sectors. Matters relating to taxation come under the Ministry of Finance. In March 2005, the Ministry of Education appointed a taskforce to coordinate and activate measures in different administrative sectors for carrying out the proposals of the one-person commission.

4.3. Netherlands[16]

Authorities in the Netherlands have displayed a readiness to employ tax policy as a tool for furthering the government's strong support for investment in human capital. Over the past decade they have introduced deductions intended to enhance incentives for employers to increase overall investment in learning-related activity, to encourage training for particular target groups, and to encourage individuals to save for learning-related purposes. Since 2002 fiscal pressures, doubts about the efficacy of some measures, and changing priorities have forced the government to cancel some of these and other initiatives.

Treatment of revenues

In the Netherlands, certain types of education are tax-exempt. These types are defined as education provided by schools financed or recognised by the government or recognised private schools. VAT exemption also applies to music, dance and drama education for individuals under the age of 21. In practice, all (commercial) distance education courses are also free of VAT, including creative courses.

Treatment of expenditure

Educational expenses are defined as expenses of a training course or study taken by the individual for the purpose of obtaining employment and of home ownership.[17] Expenses in excess of EUR 500 are deductible, up to a maximum of EUR 15 000. In 2002, the tax expenditure for individual educational expenses (*Aftrek studiekosten*) was EUR 87 million.

---

16. Based on material submitted by Sonja Jansen, CINOP.

17. In the Dutch income tax law, training was first mentioned when the term training allowance (*scholingsaftrek*) was introduced in the 1964 Corporate Income Tax Act. In order to define what is acceptable under tax law, the Dutch government published several explanatory notes. In case there is any doubt, the tax inspector decides what is accepted or not. In some cases, a judge is asked to decide.

The definition of training is different for individuals (income tax) and organisations (corporate tax). For individuals, training and education aimed at providing income in either a current or future job is accepted within the income tax system according to the Income Tax Act 2001, article 6.27-6.30. For organisations, the tax deduction on training in Corporate Income Tax law is bound to the following restrictions:

- *Guidance*: only job and/or career-related guidance provided by a (commercial) training provider and financed by the individual or employer is allowed.

- *Training intentions*: all training activities have to do with training for jobs or income. Job and career-related training costs are deductible within certain margins.

- *Training activities*: the kind of training that is recognised by Dutch tax law is job or career-related classroom courses; internal company activities to train own employees; exchange projects between organisations.

- *Level of training activities*: in order to stimulate employers to encourage low skilled workers reaching the so-called start qualification (level 2, Act on Vocational Training), an extra 20% of the training costs can be deducted from corporate tax.

- *Conditions*: tax deduction for child care is not related to training activities but to work in general.

- *Tools*: only study books are accepted for tax deduction.

If an employee has incurred training costs, he/she is allowed to withdraw money (free of tax) from his/her registered employee savings schemes (under which employees can set aside pre-tax earnings in a savings account reserved for specified purposes). However these costs must relate to the employee's current job or future paid employment. Costs of congresses, seminars, excursions and study visits qualify as well. Under the income tax law, a specific measure exists for employees saving for sabbatical leave. If a collective arrangement exists to save time or money for extra time off (for example for study purposes), employees do not have to pay taxes for these premiums. Employees can save up to 10% of their gross wages per year to pay for educational leave. The total time off is not allowed to exceed one year. When the amounts reserved are paid out, they are taxed as ordinary income to individuals.

For employers there are a number of targeted provisions concerning the treatment of learning-related expenditure:

- For employees younger than 25 years, earning less than 130% of the legal minimum wage and working at least 36 hours a week, employers can count expenditure against the wage tax and national insurance taxes up to a limit of EUR 2 400.
- For Ph.D. students engaged in research within the employer's company the tax deduction for education expenses applies for a maximum of 48 months in case of a full-time research.
- For formerly unemployed workers who are under 23 and participate in special courses that award a diploma at entry-level qualification level 2, employers can credit the expenditure against the wage tax and national insurance taxes up to a limit of EUR 1 529.

Non-profit organisations (that have no profits from which to deduct training costs) are allowed to decrease the wage tax by 12% of the training costs. If the training costs are less than EUR 124 000, this percentage is 19% for the first EUR 30 000. For employees older than 40 years, an extra 14% can be deducted. Seven per cent of the costs paid to bring an employee up to start qualification level can also be deducted.[18] The maximum total deduction for an organisation is EUR 794 115 per year.[19]

In 1998, a new tax law was implemented introducing three tax deductions (Leuven and Oosterbeek, 2000) for expenditure by companies on the work-related training of employees[20] with the following effects:

- A general extra[21] deduction of training expenditure from the taxable profits: 20% of the costs for training.
- If the total amount of training costs does not exceed EUR 124 000, the training deduction will be increased by 20% over the first EUR 30 000 (an extra encouragement for small-sized companies).
- Employers can claim an extra 20% tax deduction when they train employees aged 40 or older.[22]
- If the training is aimed at bringing the employee at start qualification level, the deduction is increased by an extra 20 percentage points (to a total of 140%).
- If all the other extra deductions apply, the maximum total deduction may total 70%.
- The total amount of the training deduction may be EUR 2 390 000 per company.[23]

---

18. "Wet Vermindering Afdracht loonbelasting en premie voor de volksverzekeringen (WVA), art 5a" and "Miljoenennota 2003".

19. "Wijzigingen in de belastingheffing met ingang van 1 januari 2002, Persbericht Nr 01/335", Den Haag, 13 December 2001.

20. This measure can also be applied in case of temporary workers.

21. Training expenditure is already deducted when profits are calculated.

22. In 2003 it is no longer possible to make use of this tax measure.

23. "Wijzigingen in de belastingheffing met ingang van 1 januari 2002, Persbericht Nr 01/335", Den Haag, 13 December 2001.

In 2002 the tax expenditure on these various measures exceeded EUR 600 million: tax deduction for education (*Afdrachtvermindering onderwijs*) – EUR 231 million; tax deduction for training in the non-profit sector (*Afdrachtvermindering scholing*) – EUR 98 million; extra training allowances for employers (*Scholingsaftrek werkgevers*) – EUR 280 million. The Dutch government cancelled the complete training deduction measure effective 1 January 2004.

In the Netherlands, most of the collective labour agreements rule that a compulsory payment (wage levy) must be made to the industry training fund. These costs are also treated as training costs in the tax system.

Entrepreneurs can receive several subsidies and contributions for the training of their employees. Training costs less specific subsidies must be used to calculate the final allowance. In addition, payments from employees to the employer for training and deferrals must be deducted from the training costs.

In 2003 and 2004 there were a number of adjustments made to eliminate special provisions for education and training:

- On 1 January 2003, premium savings accounts and profit-sharing measures were abolished. The employee saving schemes continued in 2003. The tax-free amount an employee may save was reduced.

- Since 1 January 2003, the extra deduction for training costs made for 40-plus employees was cancelled for both profit and non-profit organisations.

- For employees older than 40 years, the extra 14% can no longer be deducted either.[24]

- Tax allowances training for both profit and not-for-profit organisations were cancelled because the government concluded that the measures did not stimulate training participation but merely rewarded organisations that would have participated in training anyway.

Recent discussions and tax measures evaluated

The Netherlands has experienced difficulties with the definition of post-initial learning in relation to deductible costs. Since no adequate definition can be given, some persons argue that the training deduction has to be abolished. The tax deduction was abolished in 2004 because of provisional evidence of minor impacts on training participation[25] (a formal evaluation of the effect of those measures never took place). Recently the Dutch government decided to implement as from 1 January 2006 the so-called *Levensloopregeling* (career break scheme). This scheme gives citizens the opportunity to set aside before-tax earnings for sabbatical, care or educational leave.[26]

---

24. "Wet Vermindering Afdracht loonbelasting en premie voor de volksverzekeringen (WVA), art 15a" and "Miljoenennota 2003".

25. See also "Waarom de fiscus zich niet met scholing moet bemoeien", H. Oosterbeek, 16 November 2001.

26. In mid-2002, the Dutch Ministry of Education decided to continue the Individual Learning Account experiment within the eight existing pilots. This experiment started in February 2001. The second round started in November 2002 and ended on 31 December 2003. This provided EUR 1.1 million for 1 300 new learning accounts in addition to the 1 200 that already existed. The results confirmed the usefulness of demand-led incentives for lifelong learning. However it was not clear that such approaches would work for all groups, including the poorly qualified. For this reason another experiment with individual learning accounts (using experimental and control groups) is being launched in 2005 to test for effects of such mechanisms on less educated persons. First results are expected in 2007. No special tax measures exist for these accounts.

4.4. Tax policy and lifelong learning: policy by accident

The preceding overview of experience in Austria, Finland and the Netherlands, key elements of which are summarised in Table 4.7, suggests that regardless of the expressed intentions of (central government) tax policy with regard to investment in human capital, there are differences across countries in the treatment of expenditure on such investment, and differences within countries regarding the stance of tax policy towards investment by individuals compared to employers. Moreover, there would appear to be some ambiguity regarding the tax situation of public/non-profit education and training providers compared to for-profit providers that could have a material affect on the cost structure of each.

Table 4.7 Overview of main features of tax policy regarding investment in human capital
Selected countries: Austria, Finland, Netherlands

Country (*ratio of tax expenditure to education expenditure*)	Treatment of revenues		Treatment of expenditure	
	Public/ non-profit providers[1]	For-profit providers	Employers	Individuals
Austria (< 0.5%)	Exempt from VAT	Not exempt from VAT or income tax	120% of expenses are deductible from earnings; companies not earning a profit are entitled to a credit equal to 6% of expenditure that can be received as a subsidy or applied to payroll taxes	100% of direct costs of learning related to present or future employment are deductible from earnings
Finland (2%)	Exempt from VAT. Exempt from income tax	General education and training exempt from VAT. Not exempt from income tax	100% of expenses associated with staff development are deductible from earnings	Standard deduction of EUR 590 (2003) from earnings when individuals participate in work-related education/training. Costs of education/training that raises qualifications and prepares for new duties are treated as taxable income
Netherlands (3%)	Exempt from VAT	General education and training exempt from VAT. Not exempt from income tax	120% of expenses associated with education/training can be deducted from earnings; for non-profit entities, 12-19% of costs can be deducted from social charges	Education expenses up to a maximum of EUR 15 000 can be deducted from earnings

1. Institutions designated by government as serving education purposes.

Source: Secretariat calculations based on Jansen (2003).

The tax treatment of expenditure by employers is one area in which there appears to be important differences between the few countries considered here. Employers uniformly deduct education and training-related costs from taxable profits as a cost of doing business. But Austria and the Netherlands have deliberately created extra incentives for employers to invest in training by allowing them to deduct something more than 100% of such costs. They also happen to be two countries that provide extra incentives for companies to invest in R&D. Finland does neither. But it is not clear whether such consistency matters for the behaviour of firms with respect to investment in training (and other "intangible assets" such as R&D), and/or ultimately, for competitiveness. The Austrian initiatives are too recent to be evaluated. Certain initiatives were evaluated in the Netherlands, though too soon to provide an authoritative view of their effectiveness and impacts.

For individuals recent initiatives have made it easier to deduct costs of education and training beyond that which is required for current employment. The recent initiatives relax earlier policies that restricted deductions to training that was specifically required to remain in the job in which individuals were employed. Individuals now can deduct expenses associated with learning required for current as well as future employment, either with the same or different employers. Although the new provisions still exclude education and training that is not related to employment, they move in the direction of better aligning the tax treatment of learning-related expenditure with the consensus view as to the importance of broad increases in investment in human capital. However the application of this line of thinking is far from uniform even among the limited number of countries considered here. In Finland, for example, in the case of an individual following a degree programme that is paid for by an employer, the value of the subsidy would be treated as taxable income to the individual.

The treatment of revenues appears to be fairly uniform with respect to payment of value-added and/or sales taxes on the fees paid for education and training services. Such services are exempt or subject to a comparatively low rate, whether provided by public or private providers. However it is an area in which the wider pursuit of lifelong learning could give rise to certain ambiguities. In the Netherlands, for example, there are higher VAT rates imposed for leisure courses, as compared to vocational courses, begging the question of whether the distinction is always clear. In Austria, for-profit providers are exempt from paying VAT provided their programmes "are comparable to those of public schools", raising the question of how "comparability" is evaluated and whether this risks penalising innovations by for-profit providers if it makes their services too different from the public fare. There appears to be more uniformity among the countries considered with respect to the tax treatment of income by for-profit providers compared to other providers, with the former subject to corporate tax and the latter exempt.

5. CONCLUSION

This chapter started by recognising that economic and fiscal constraints are important, but not the only barriers to implementation of lifelong learning. It then set out to explore the issues that might arise as lifelong learning is implemented in an environment in which pre-existing tax policies influence decision making and investment choices by individuals and employers. It focuses on decisions and choices related to lifelong learning for adults because that is where the issues are most immediate and most relevant.

"Lifelong learning" has evolved as a policy initiative that was pushed initially by education ministries, then adopted by labour ministries, and subsequently pushed in tandem with other government policies aimed at facilitating the transition into the knowledge society. It is an initiative that has attracted broad support because the stakes are widely shared throughout government and by social partners. But the hopes and ambitions that have lent important political impetus to lifelong learning have been dampened to some degree by the difficulties of effectively coordinating the diverse policies that impact on the implementation of lifelong learning. These difficulties range from complex – developing pedagogies that can be integrated with work – to the mundane – providing classroom facilities during evening hours. The difficulties that are inherent in some of these issues are compounded by the fact that remedies and progress hinge to a high degree on coordinating action across different policy portfolios.

Tax policy appears to be one area where debate and initiatives have been largely unconnected with developments in lifelong learning. There is a multitude of reasons for this. The dialogue between education and finance ministries has been preoccupied with the issues related to the budget of a large, comparatively stable sector of public spending. Financing issues have been straightforward. The link with the economy has been taken as given – important enough to justify a dominant public role and high levels of expenditure, and stable enough to escape the kind of scrutiny that might open underlying assumptions to scrutiny. Tax policy has been preoccupied first and foremost with raising revenue for all of government. Beyond that there are conflicting views as to whether tax policy should be wielded as a tool to influence economic behaviour. Insofar as tax policy is shaped to steer behaviour such as investment choices, education and training and human capital investment have not been deliberate targets of policy. The emergence of lifelong learning as part of the broader shift to a knowledge society puts this past pattern of policy making under pressure, raising questions as to whether current policy sends the right signals, and whether tax policy can and should be used as a tool to further investment in human capital.

As a result it would appear that presently the stance of central government tax policy *vis à vis* lifelong learning is accidental, perhaps anachronistic. Judging from the experience of the three countries whose experience is discussed above, as well as from political debates among policy makers and stakeholders[27] it would appear that:

• Current policy varies across countries; within countries there are notable differences between individuals and employers regarding the tax treatment of human capital investments.

• The objectives (expressed or implicit) of such policies are not always consistent with the stated objectives of countries to encourage investment in lifelong learning, or the principles that guide tax policy.

• There is limited evidence of whether tax policy has an impact on investment in human capital, and whether the observed variations between countries in their policies are of any consequence.

This chapter did not set out to draw conclusions about how tax policy might be changed to enhance the financial means and economic incentives to invest in lifelong learning, or the desirability of using tax policy for such purposes. Such judgments require at a minimum:

• Information from additional countries describing the tax treatment of learning-related expenditure and revenue under current policy.

• Evidence of the impact such policy has on aggregate levels of provision of, and investment in, lifelong learning.

• Evidence of the impact of such policy on particular groups, such as those with low earnings, and of the conditions which increase or decrease such impacts.

---

27. Most recently at the international conference on co-financing lifelong learning that was held in Bonn in October 2003. See OECD (2004a).

However it might be inferred from the material presented here that regardless of whether tax policy *should* be brought to bear as a tool for facilitating national strategies for lifelong learning, a more comprehensive stocktaking would be useful. Further discussion and debate would be facilitated if there were available for more countries additional descriptive information concerning the stance of current tax policy regarding investment in lifelong learning, as well as evaluative evidence of the impact of such policy, both in aggregate terms and with respect to the distribution of learning opportunities. Indicators of current tax policy might make it easier to carry out comparative analysis that would shed light on these issues.

When it comes to remedies such as changes in tax policy ministries of finance have ultimate authority. But there is a broad circle of actors – governmental and social partners – that have a direct stake in the answer to the question of whether tax policy has an impact on levels of investment in lifelong learning and the distribution of learning opportunities. Practically speaking, it is incumbent on ministries of education – the ones that have traditionally assumed primary responsibility for human capital development – to take a proactive role in debates on tax policy to ensure its consistency with governmental policy on learning, investment and innovation. The outcome of developments may have material consequences for the capacity of societies to develop coherent policies for lifelong learning.

The tax and investment issues that arise in connection with lifelong learning for adults are not the only unsettled issues that arise in connection with lifelong learning. Insofar as lifelong learning succeeds in making it easier for individuals to spread certain aspects of their learning over the lifetime (rather than undertaking the maximum amount of formal education *before* entering the labour market), the question arises as to whether it is important to harmonise the treatment of learning-related expenditure across the lifetime (not just focusing on expenditure incurred during adulthood). For example, given the evidence of the strong positive impact of early childhood education on subsequent schooling experience on the one hand, and the limited capacity of government to pay the full cost of extra capacity at this level, one also can ask whether tax policy might play a role in strengthening the incentives and means for private financing in this area. The fact that these questions are beyond the scope of this chapter does not diminish their importance. They too merit further attention in the future; and here again, education ministries will have to argue the case for addressing them.

References

Immervoll, H. (2004), "Average and Marginal Effective Tax Rates Facing Workers in the EU: A Micro-level Analysis of Levels, Distributions and Driving Factors", OECD Social, Employment and Migration Working Paper No. 19, OECD, Paris, December.

Jansen, S. (2003), "Tax Treatment: Comparison of Tax Expenditure and Tax Treatment of Post-initial Learning Activities in Austria, Finland and the Netherlands", CINOP, Utrecht, prepared for the workshop on "Tax Policy and Lifelong Learning" that was held as part of the International Conference "A Systemic Approach to Co-financing Lifelong Learning", held in October 2003 in Bonn, Germany (available at *www.oecd.org*).

Leuven, E. and H. Oosterbeek (2000), "Evaluating the Effect of Tax Deductions on Training", mimeo, October, *econwpa. wustl.edu*:8089/*eps/lab/papers/0205/0205001.pdf*

OECD (2000), *Where are the Resources for Lifelong Learning?*, OECD, Paris.

OECD (2001), *Economics and Finance of Lifelong Learning*, OECD, Paris.

OECD (2002a), *Education at a Glance* – OECD Indicators 2002, OECD, Paris.

OECD (2002b), *Reviews of National Policies for Education – Lifelong Learning in Norway*, OECD, Paris.

OECD (2003a), *Beyond Rhetoric: Adult Learning Policies and Practices*, OECD, Paris.

OECD (2003b), "Upgrading Workers' Skills and Competencies", *Employment Outlook* 2003, OECD, Paris, Chapter 5.

OECD (2003c), "Taking Stock of Co-finance Mechanisms" (updated 28 April), *www.oecd.org*

OECD (2003d), "Strategies for Sustainable Investment in Adult Lifelong Learning", *Education Policy Analysis* 2003, OECD, Paris, Chapter 4.

OECD (2004a), *Co-financing Lifelong Learning: Towards a Systemic Approach*, OECD, Paris.

OECD (2004b), "Improving Skills for More and Better Jobs: Does Training Make a Difference?", *Employment Outlook* 2004, OECD, Paris, Chapter 4.

OECD (2004c), *Taxing Wages*, OECD, Paris.

OECD Directorate for Science, Technology and Industry (2002), *Entrepreneurship and Growth: Tax Issues*, OECD, Paris, February.

OECD and US Department of Education (1999), *How Adults Learn*, US Government Printing Office, Washington DC.

Van den Noord, P. and C. Heady (2001), "Surveillance of Tax Policies: A Synthesis of Findings in Economic Surveys", Economics Department Working Paper No. 303, OECD, Paris.

ANNEX: Recent education policy developments

This annex contains summaries of recent education policy developments. Countries were invited to submit the summaries organised around the six strategic priorities that now structure the OECD's work in education. A number of countries chose to do so. The maximum length was 400 words per country. Due to space constraints, the entries have not been able to cover all significant policy developments. The emphasis was on outlining major education policy developments that have occurred recently or which are being implemented, and which are likely to be of most interest to an international audience. The entries have been edited to provide a consistent format and to observe space constraints.

Summaries were provided by 16 OECD countries: Australia; Austria; Belgium (French Community); Czech Republic; Denmark; Finland; France; Hungary; Japan; Korea; Luxembourg; Norway; Poland; Portugal; Slovak Republic; and the United Kingdom. In addition, contributions were provided by Israel and the Russian Federation, which have observer status on the OECD Education Committee.

AUSTRALIA

Promoting lifelong learning and improving its linkages with other socio-economic policies

The Australian government has produced a report to assess the long-term sustainability of government policies, including education, taking into account the financial implications of demographic change. It is engaged in a national consultation on adult learning to address the challenges presented by Australia's ageing population, particularly in rural and regional Australia.

Evaluating and improving outcomes of education

Australian governments and the non-government school sector have established national key performance measures for reporting against the National Goals for Schooling. There is an annual full-cohort literacy and numeracy testing, and three-yearly sample assessments of science, ICT and civics and citizenship education. To support the National Goals, a National Literacy and Numeracy Plan has been implemented. To improve Indigenous students' outcomes, reforms to the Australian Indigenous Education Programmes will from 2005 direct extra funding to schools in remote areas and will support the involvement of Indigenous parents and communities in school education. The data collected through national benchmarking facilitate targeted assistance.

Promoting quality teaching

Under the Australian Government Quality Teacher Programme $159 million is being provided to improve the skills and understanding of teachers, and to enhance the status of teaching. The Australian government will fund a National Institute for Quality Teaching and School Leadership to enhance the quality and status of teaching and school leadership. In July 2003, the Ministerial Council on Education, Employment, Training and Youth Affairs (MCEETYA) endorsed a National Framework for Professional Standards for Teaching and is exploring nationally-aligned entry-level standards for teachers.

Rethinking tertiary education in a global economy

In 2002, the Australian government conducted a review of higher education and the government announced reforms in May 2003. The package is based on sustainability, quality, equity and diversity. The Australian government has allocated funds to improve quality assurance mechanisms for offshore campuses. It has introduced an income-contingent loan scheme which provides financial support for study abroad and exchange.

Building social cohesion through education

Australian governments are working with Indigenous communities in a trial programme to provide more flexible programmes and services. In the trials, responsibility for the condition and well-being of Indigenous communities is shared between families, individuals, communities and governments.

Building new futures for education

Australia has developed Myfuture (*www.myfuture.edu.au*), a national internet-based careers exploration service, for individuals at every stage of life. The Australian government is working with States and Territories to develop an e-learning blueprint for schools and supports a range of other ICT initiatives.

Further information: *www.dest.gov.au/*

AUSTRIA

Promoting lifelong learning and improving its linkages with other socio-economic policies

Taking 2010, the target year of the European Union's Lisbon Declaration, as a point of reference, the Austrian government has established a lifelong learning "Taskforce LLL:2010". Its brief is to come up with strategies which give the highly fragmented system of adult education more coherence and to develop an action plan with a clear time frame and new performance indicators.

Evaluating and improving outcomes of education and promoting quality teaching

In 2003 the Education Ministry set up a Future Commission. Some of the recommendations of the commission's preliminary report were adopted by the government in June 2004. These include:

- The establishment of a system to monitor the performance and efficiency of Austria's schools.

- The introduction of testable standards for critical transition points in Austrian school careers: at age 10 – the end of primary school; and at age 14 – the end of lower secondary education. These were to be piloted in 100 schools from September 2004.

- More accountability and personal responsibility of teachers and principals for the quality of learning in the classroom. One key policy is the establishment of a Leadership Academy to upgrade the professional competence of school principals and of other persons responsible for school management (*www.klassezukunft.at*).

Rethinking tertiary education in a global economy

Since the university reform of 2002, the diversification of higher education has gained momentum:

- An increasing number of study programmes are changing over to the three-stage structure recommended by the European Union's Bologna Declaration.

- The non-university sector (*Fachhochschulen*) has become a highly attractive vocationally-focused part-time study option alongside employment.

- By 2007 the transformation of the hitherto post-secondary teacher training academies into proper higher education institutions should be completed.

Building new futures for education

Early in 2003, the Ministry of Education commissioned a group to analyse the Austrian school system and to propose policies for its improvement. In October 2003, the commission's report was made available and stakeholders in education were invited to express their opinions. In addition, a series of regional conferences was held to provide opportunities for debate and dialogue. A ministerial taskforce will integrate the final experts' report, the public responses to it, proposals made at the regional conferences, and an already existing White Paper on Quality Assurance into an Education Plan 2010.

BELGIUM (French Community)

The French Community of Belgium is a federated entity whose responsibilities include, inter alia, education policy for the French-speaking part of the country (the Walloon Region and the bilingual Region of Brussels-Capital). In the 2002-03 school year, there were 485 263 children enrolled in basic education (kindergarten and primary schools); 359 809 in secondary education and 141 924 in higher education (university and non-university).

The most important reform of compulsory education (6 to 18 years) took place in July 1997 with the adoption of legislation relating to the missions of the education system. For the first time these missions were clearly defined and, as a result, the Parliament of the French Community adopted specifications of core skills which all children must have mastered at key stages in their school career. In tandem with this reform, a governing body, in the form of a commission, was set up for the education system.

Besides these changes, a number of legislative or regulatory initiatives have been taken to ensure a level playing field for social emancipation, notably in the form of differentiated funding for teaching establishments, through implementation of a policy of positive discrimination, and through creation of a special advisory and support system for non-French speaking immigrant children.

In the higher education sector, attention should above all be drawn to the recent structural reform designed to integrate Belgium in the European Higher Education Area (Bologna Process) through the creation of an agency to assess the quality of teaching in this sector.

Further information may be found at the following websites: *www.cfwb.be, www.enseignement.be, www.restode.cfwb.be*

CZECH REPUBLIC

Developments in the Czech Republic have focused on two priorities of the White Paper (2000) incorporated in the new Educational Act.

Curriculum reforms have introduced a system of multi-level educational programmes based on the concept of key competences. At the national level, both an overarching state education programme and framework educational programmes (FEP) for each level of education and field of study are being developed. Schools will create their own educational programmes based on the respective frameworks. The framework for pre-primary education has already been implemented. Frameworks for primary and lower secondary education were to be approved by the end of 2004. The framework for upper secondary general education (*gymnasia*) is under the pilot testing at schools, and is to be approved in 2006. Frameworks for various types of upper secondary education technical and vocational schools will follow.

The increased autonomy of schools is being matched by gradually establishing a comprehensive evaluation system. At the level of the student, a bank of test items and tests is being developed which will enable the educational attainment of all pupils to be assessed at key stages (5th and 9th forms). Reform of the *Maturita*, or upper secondary final examination, is already under way, and is to be introduced in 2009. The reform of the final examination for vocational education has just started. At the level of schools, self-evaluation will be introduced and closely linked to external evaluation by the School Inspectorate. At the level of the educational system, the focus is on better linking the outcomes of international surveys to additional national surveys and other available data, and on setting in place a regional level corresponding to the new structure of school governance.

DENMARK

Recognition of prior learning

A policy paper on enhanced validation and recognition of prior learning was prepared for submission to Parliament in 2004. The initiative follows the reform of the Danish career-guidance and counselling system implemented the previous year and includes: the provision of new comprehensive options for education; quality assurance; and enhanced concurrence between education and social and leisure time activity.

Finalisation of a national competence account

The aim is for the account to form a basis for locating strengths – and weaknesses – in national competences. At the same time it is to form a basis for political initiatives in the sphere of competence. The national competence account will also contribute to public debate on Danish competences. The first account was published in the autumn of 2004.

Enhanced internationalisation

In April 2004 a policy paper entitled Enhanced Internationalisation of Danish Education was submitted to, and endorsed by, Parliament. The paper, which presents a comprehensive policy covering the entire education and research sector, addresses the challenges of globalisation and the emergence of a knowledge-based society.

The policy includes measures to enhance: the international dimension in the curriculum; the mobility of students and teachers; the use of ICT; increasing opportunities for institutions in transnational co-operation and competition; and increasing Denmark's involvement in international co-operation and comparisons.

Policy implications of the pilot review to examine quality and equity

The decision to engage Denmark in the OECD-led review on quality and equity in school outcomes was motivated by two reasons: the modest Danish results in PISA 2000; and the fact that the impact of the social background of pupils on school outcomes apparently is significantly stronger in Denmark than in the countries it usually compares itself to.

Participation in the review must in itself be regarded as a policy development. Consensus has now been established that the Danish primary and lower secondary school system must develop a new culture of evaluation to raise standards, and to create a platform for early intervention to address the needs of pupils with modest learning disabilities. The Minister for Education has initiated four working-groups, including all major stakeholders, to develop recommendations for further initiatives. The reform of initial teacher training that is being prepared at the moment will be influenced by the results of the review.

In addition, Parliament has agreed on a reform of general upper secondary education that will be implemented from August 2005. Additional information and downloading of publications in English: *www.uvm.dk*

FINLAND

Building social cohesion through education

Today, children spend more time without the care of a safe adult than before, and the pressures to balance family and working life and children's care and school life are constantly growing. The demand for before- and after-school activities clearly exceeds the supply. According to studies, 75% of parents whose children are starting school consider their child to need guided activities before or after school. To improve the situation, Finland promulgated an Act on 1 August 2004 to improve government financing of these activities as well as their quality. Government financing will be available to activities provided for first- and second-year pupils (age 7-8) and for pupils with special needs. The aim is that the provision will meet the need indicated by parents. From the beginning of August 2004, about 60% of first-year and one third of second-year pupils will have access to organised before- and after-school activities. Most of the activities will be provided by sports clubs, other civic organisations and congregations. One third of the activities will be provided by local authorities. The financing will mostly come from government grants and fees to be paid by parents. For more information: *www.minedu.fi*

FRANCE

In 2003-04, there were two major events that mark French educational policy.

The first was the national debate on the future of French education, launched in September 2003 at the request of the President of the Republic and the Prime Minister, and coordinated by a commission attached to the Ministry of National Education. Its objective was threefold:

- To encourage all French citizens (parents, students, national education employees, economic actors, local and national elected officials, citizens, etc.) to speak out about the big issues in education, from nursery school up to entry into higher education.

- To arrive at a common diagnosis (a summary of the debates has been published under the title *Le miroir des débats*, available at *www.education.gouv.fr*).

- To contribute to government reflection in preparation for a guideline Bill submitted to Parliament in the fall of 2004 to establish the objectives of schooling for tomorrow.

The second was the 15 March 2004 Act regulating the wearing of religious symbols or dress in public elementary, junior high and high schools. This act reaffirms the principles of secularity and freedom which, in the French republican tradition, guarantee neutrality in schools and the integration of all into the national community (the circular specifying how this new legislation is to be enforced is available at *www.education.gouv.fr*).

Other priorities – new or renewed – include the following:

- Improving mastery of basic skills in primary schools (reading, writing, arithmetic), as well as of foreign languages and both information and communication technologies.

- Diversifying training opportunities and career paths in junior high and high schools, and reaffirming the importance of technical training and its relation to general education in order to reduce the number of young people leaving the educational system without qualifications.

- Reinforcing lifelong learning and the implementation of a system which takes professional experience into account.

- Preventing violence in schools, developing citizenship education and supporting young people's involvement.

- Pursuing at university level the implementation of a European degree-masters-doctorate programme, encouraging student mobility, and enhancing the international appeal of French higher education.

- Promoting scientific studies and careers.

HUNGARY

Promoting lifelong learning and improving its linkages with other socio-economic policies

Links between education and other policy areas were strengthened in the process of creating the National Development Plan for 2004-06, and through the preparation of the Human Resource Development Operational Programme. A committee of relevant ministers has recently been set up to provide a whole-of-government approach in social policy issues, and to examine the impact and the social consequences of decisions. See: *www.fmm.gov.hu/main.php?folderID=3442*

Evaluating and improving outcomes of education

A new competence assessment system was introduced in 2001. This covers all members of specific age groups and allows schools to compare their achievement and progress with others. The results help to identify pedagogical, management, organisational and socio-economic factors leading to good or bad performance. Further information: *www.om.hu/education*

Promoting quality teaching

Initial teacher training programmes are being unified and standardised, and a development programme is supporting the implementation of competence-based education. Developing curricula, programme packages, teachers' skills and raising awareness of innovative practices is the focal point of the programme. In 2002 teachers' basic salary was raised by 50% and various bonuses were introduced to reward high quality teaching. Further information: *www.om.hu/education*

Rethinking tertiary education in a global economy

In 2003, the government published its medium-term strategy for the development of the higher education system to increase its competitiveness and adaptability and to strengthen its regional role and its research and development capacity. Readjusting the training structure according to the Bologna Process is under way. A number of measures are planned to improve institutions' management structure, quality assurance systems, human resource policies and co-operation with economic players. Further information: *www.fmm. gov.hu/main.php?folderID=3442*

Building social cohesion through education

New laws to eliminate segregation and promote non-discriminatory education are currently being implemented. A fairer distribution of financial support to reduce inequalities, and an additional per capita grant for integrated education, were introduced recently. The National Educational Integration Network is a horizontal learning and tutorial system that assists the adaptation and implementation of inclusive educational programmes. A methodological databank is being established, and programme packages for preventing early school-leaving are being developed. Further information: *www.om.hu/education*

Building new futures for education

The Ministry of Education has launched a programme called Schools of the 21st Century to modernise the learning environment in schools and to adjust their premises to the requirements of e-learning.
Further information: *www.oki.hu/article.php?kod=english-Policy.html*

ISRAEL

During the last two years, Israel has begun to implement a core curriculum, differential primary school budgeting and early measurement and evaluation testing. It faces the challenges of immigrant absorption, religious and sectoral divisions, social and economic gaps, the need to equalise the position and status of its Arab minority and severe budget cuts in recent years. In September 2003, Israel appointed a task force to evaluate its education system and to recommend a programme for structural, organisational and pedagogical change. Its interim recommendations were published in May 2004. They focus upon: strengthening early school stages and public education; instituting a full school day; narrowing gaps; measuring and evaluating students' progress and achievements; improving the teaching profession and its status; restoring school autonomy; result-oriented management; decentralising management; accountability and transparency; concentrating resources; and streamlined and realistic budgeting. The most far-reaching change will be the institution of a full school day, five days a week, instead of six half days. Middle schools will be abolished to reduce the number of transitions in a student's career. Schools will have greater pedagogic, budgetary, and administrative autonomy, as well as choice of personnel, including educational staff. The teaching profession will be improved through higher entry standards, internship and licensing examinations. Some training colleges will be upgraded, others will be closed. Teachers will take on educational tasks now performed by other instructional personnel. To compensate them for the longer hours that they will be required to work, there will be a significant increase in teachers' salaries.

Standards will be set for all school principals' functions and training. Minimal acceptance requirements for a principal will include a Master's degree, educational experience and management training. The hiring and firing of principals will be conducted by a committee headed by the district educational administration director. There will be guidance for new principals. Principals' salary scales will be separate from teachers' salaries; training programmes for principals will be developed.

Measurable annual goals will be defined for every school and an annual report will be published, including internal and external evaluation. Management of the school system will be decentralised. Resources will be streamlined, with an "educational basket" to be set for each child, pooling all necessary resources. Clear budgeting formulae are to be set to allocate the financial burden between the government and local authorities, while taking into consideration the authorities' strengths.

JAPAN

In 2004, Japan pursued the steady implementation of the plan to reform the quotas of educational personnel to ensure the number of teachers necessary for teaching according to individual student needs, such as those based on their level of maturity. Efforts will be made for further realisation of "lessons that are easy to understand". This will be done by positive assistance to each school and/or Board of Education to improve "definite academic ability" in all children. Improvement will be sought through conducting practical research into teaching methods; developing teaching materials at core schools in order to promote instruction responding to the individual; and by dispatching human resources active in the front line to raise motivation for learning.

To improve teacher quality Japan has been implementing the necessary policy measures systematically through teacher education, recruitment and in-service training. Also by carrying out wide-ranging and systematic personnel exchanges, Japan is trying to eliminate regional differences in teacher acquisition, offer equal opportunities for education, and both improve and maintain a nationwide educational standard. In addition, the following measures are being implemented to improve the quality of teachers: performance assessments of teachers and treatment which reflects their efforts; strict handling of teachers with problems in teaching; and employment of working people at school.

From April 2004, incorporation of Japan's national universities as independent organisations took place. Universities' responsibility for knowledge creation is becoming more and more important to Japan, which is aiming to develop as an education- and culture-oriented nation and a nation that creates science and technology. The incorporation of national universities is being carried out with the aim of creating appealing national universities that are rich in individuality, thereby allowing Japanese national universities to better fulfil their responsibilities. In this sense, demands are on universities to advance and revitalise their education and research activities in order to meet the expectations of the public and society. Each national university since incorporation has been working actively toward reform in the fields of education and research, contributions to revitalising the community, co-operation with industry, and management systems. In 2003, a new professional graduate school system was introduced with the aim of cultivating human resources that can be employed in advanced, professional jobs in every sector of society and to fulfil the function of nurturing of human resources with specialised knowledge and skills. The Central Education Council's Subcommittee on Universities has been deliberating on a future vision for higher education.

KOREA

Promoting lifelong learning and improving its linkages with other socio-economic policies

The Ministry of Education and Human Resources Development launched the School Enterprise Promotion Support Project in 2004 to: support the establishment and management of companies within universities, colleges, vocational high schools and other vocational education institutions; use company facilities for on-site training and teaching; promote technology transfer; and contribute to school finances through profits. Companies shall be established through close ties with specific curriculum fields as organisations under the school structure. They will carry out manufacture, processing, repairs, sales, and services. The system begins in 2004 and will be operated until 2008.

Evaluating and improving outcomes of education

Since 2002, the Ministry of Education and Human Resources Development has conducted an annual assessment of reading, writing and arithmetic among approximately 3% of 3rd grade students, along with a survey of background variables. Metropolitan and provincial offices of education encourage schools to conduct independent assessments to identify students with inadequate basic scholastic development. The assessment items are based on those in the national test. Results are provided to metropolitan and provincial offices of education and schools in the form of a report.

Rethinking tertiary education in a global economy

To sharpen universities' competitive edge, the Ministry of Education and Human Resources Development has launched programmes to: reinforce research-intensive universities; nurture science and engineering talent; implement the New University for Regional Innovation Project to stimulate regional development; stimulate industry-academic ties; encourage globalisation of university education; and build information infrastructures at universities.

The ministry is also preparing a plan to redefine the functions and roles of universities. Student quotas for national public universities in the Seoul metropolitan area will continue to decline. Universities undertaking restructuring efforts on an independent level will be given priority in administrative and financial assistance. Comprehensive measures including amendments in laws and systems are also planned.

Building social cohesion through education

A variety of policies such as special education and tuition support for low-income families have previously been implemented, but have not been well co-ordinated or comprehensive and have failed to cope with inequity. As a result the Ministry of Education and Human Resources Development is working on comprehensive plans for educational welfare. The plans for educational welfare have three major objectives: to guarantee minimum education for all; to resolve inequality; and to create an environment of welfare. The ministry plans to strengthen ties with related agencies, to establish welfare divisions at metropolitan and provincial education offices, and to encourage public participation in implementing welfare policies.

LUXEMBOURG

Luxembourg is a representative democracy in the form of a constitutional monarchy. Under the Constitution, the State is responsible for the organisation and regulation of education. The Communes play a role in managing early, preschool and primary education. Public schools are free in Luxembourg. Educational policy is implemented by the government in power. A large number of initiatives and reforms were completed in 2003. In the context of the implementation of the government's programme, an enormous project was undertaken to restructure Luxembourg schools in order to give them the necessary means and confidence to take on the challenge of giving every child a chance at academic success in an increasingly changing environment. It was necessary to begin by defining the missions of Luxembourg's schools, giving a degree of autonomy to actors in the field, and planning the kinds of administrative and partnership structures needed for modern education management. At the same time, the pedagogical work that has been in progress for several years, the aim of which is to strengthen basic education, began to be put into application. Throughout all of this, the fight against academic failure has been the top priority. The measures taken in a variety of very different areas have all been marked by the same philosophy: create opportunities for success that make it possible to avoid unnecessary failures while maintaining standards and increasing the amount of responsibility assumed by those concerned.

NORWAY

Evaluating and improving outcomes of education

A national quality assessment system for Norwegian primary and secondary schools is under development. As part of this system, national tests in reading, writing, English and mathematics will be carried out. The first national tests took place in the spring of 2004. The national tests are intended to be a source for dialogue and quality development, to be a pedagogical tool and an aid in learning and teaching, and to make it easier to follow the development of pupils and schools over a long period of time. A national web site for school assessment and development (*www.skoleporten.no*) was launched in August 2004. The purpose of the national quality assessment system is to provide information on learning outcomes, the learning environment, and the resource situation. A cross-sectoral programme for digital literacy covering the period 2004-08 was launched in March 2004 with the vision of digital literacy for all.

Promoting quality teaching

By introducing new qualification demands for applicants for teacher training colleges the government wants to make sure that the students have the academic standards and motivation deemed necessary for teachers. Higher qualification requirements for pre-school teachers who wish to become primary school teachers will also be introduced. The government has committed itself to support a substantial programme on competence building for teachers, principals and school administrators. See *www.odin.dep.no/ufd/engelsk/publ/veiledninger/045071-120012/dok-bn.html*

POLAND

In order to address the lack of a coherent lifelong learning strategy, a strategy for the development of continuing education until the year 2010 was adopted by the Council of Ministers in July 2003. It was the first document of this rank dealing with the problems of continuing education and lifelong learning in Poland. In 2003, the School Education Act was amended to define basic concepts connected with continuing education and to insert reference to continuing education and adult education and training, in both school and out-of-school forms, including distance education. In the new legislation an organisational framework of continuing education has been developed, and types of schools and institutions which provide continuing education have been defined. The proposed changes aim to facilitate the transition between the school and out-of-school systems. The provisions of the act also encompass the acquisition of vocational qualifications and titles. The 2003 amendments to the School Education Act created legal grounds for the accreditation of institutions providing continuing education in out-of-school forms in Poland. They permit schools to recognise courses completed in out-of-school forms, with the aim of confirming already acquired qualifications.

Starting from January 2004, accreditation can be awarded and withdrawn by the education superintendent of the region. However, an important role is played by a team whose task is to evaluate the work of an institution applying for accreditation. As well as the representatives of regional education authorities, the team includes representatives of employers and local labour offices. Fifty-three modular programmes have been developed so far. They constitute a new type of offer on the educational market, and their implementation has had a great impact on the quality of vocational education and training. The modular programmes enable specialised training to adjust to changes occurring on the labour market; they also help students to develop the occupational skills needed at work and contribute to the individualisation of the teaching process. They concern 25 vocations at the level of technician but are also addressed to graduates from vocational upper secondary schools, for whom it will now be possible to continue education in a shortened cycle in post-secondary schools. In addition, 27 learning kits have been developed, serving as teaching aids in particular modules.

PORTUGAL

The Portuguese Parliament approved the new Comprehensive Law on Education in May 2004. It increases compulsory schooling from 9 to 12 years in duration and introduces major changes in the general organisation of the education system. The law applies to all levels and modes of education. Among other aspects, it reinforces the complementarities between school education and vocational training, as well as the co-ordination of the ministries responsible for education policy and employment policy. This is also the objective of several initiatives undertaken lately, thus contributing at the same time to achieving social cohesion through education. Examples include launching of the national plan for the prevention of early school leaving and the reform of special education and of socio-educational support. Another is the recent creation – jointly by the Ministries of Education and of Labour – of a set of education and training courses leading to a professional qualification. The importance that is attached in Portugal to the evaluation of education results was the reason for the creation of a Bureau for Information and Evaluation of the Education System (following the process of restructuring of the Ministry of Education). It is also the reason for the revision of the rules and procedures for the evaluation of secondary education students, to be followed by change to the evaluation system for the basic education level (*www.min-edu.pt*). Reference should also be made to the approval by the Portuguese Parliament of the proposal for a new law on the autonomy of higher education institutions and a new law on their funding. These laws stem from the on-going process of rethinking the role of tertiary education in a global economy (*www.mces.gov.pt*).

RUSSIAN FEDERATION

Evaluating and improving outcomes of education

Following a government reform, responsibility for quality assurance will lie within the Federal Service for Supervision over Education and Science. It will inherit from the former ministry tools of quality control: accreditation, attestation and licensing. Development of monitoring programmes in the education system is initiated by Ministry of Education and Sciences. The goal of all monitoring programmes is to gain information on emerging changes in the education system. As to international monitoring of secondary education outcomes, Russia has participated in the PISA survey since its inception. The results of PISA 2000 are being widely discussed now. The data of PISA 2003 were analysed for presentation in December 2004.

Promoting quality teaching

A measure to promote the quality of teaching is the creation of the all-Russian information portals system. The federal target programme "Development of a common education information area" will be completed in 2005. A federal programme to restructure rural schools is aimed at promoting quality and equity in education for disadvantaged territories. In addition a national programme "Informatisation of schools", managed by the Ministry of Education and Sciences and the Ministry of Telecommunications and Informatisation is to be completed in 2010.

Rethinking tertiary education in a global economy

Russia joined the Bologna Declaration on higher education in September 2003 and by 2010 the transition to a two-tier degree structure should be completed. The objective is specified as one of the ultimate goals of the country's educational reforms. At present about two-thirds of Russian higher education institutions practice a two-tier educational system, and the ECT system is introduced in the leading universities.

Building social cohesion through education

The education reform programme aims to alleviate the transitional barriers between secondary and tertiary education and to promote equity in higher education. The introduction of a Unified National Test (UNT) is a step toward enhancing the choices of learners and building social cohesion. UNT is an assessment of school leavers' knowledge, administered at their graduation from secondary education. It is an external quality control tool of the secondary schools' education. The UNT results are used for applications to, and enrolment in, tertiary education institutions. UNT will become compulsory in 2006.

Building new futures for education

Amalgamation of the Ministry of Sciences and the Ministry of Education in March 2004 has provided a stimulus to the programme aimed at integration of research and education.

SLOVAK REPUBLIC

In June 2002, the Parliament of the Slovak Republic adopted a national programme to improve the country's education system over a ten-to-15-year period (the MILENIUM project). Its implementation schedule until 2006 is based upon the following basic strategic priorities: reform and modernisation of the goals and content of education; development of integrated diagnostic information and advisory systems; reform of high school graduation; optimisation of the range and institutional structure of the regional school system; quality care, monitoring and evaluation of education results; improving working conditions for teachers; and development of continuous education as part of lifelong learning.

Evaluating and improving outcomes of education

National measurements of the performance of students graduating from primary schools have been carried out (from 2003), and a new form of secondary school graduation exams introduced from 2001. At the school level, from 2004 school headmasters have been required to submit annual reports to school boards and to establishing organisations on education activities, results and conditions. At the system level the main school inspector submits to the minister (and the minister submits to the government and to the Parliament) a report on the state and level of education in the Slovak Republic for each relevant school year with proposals, recommendations and modifications according to the findings of the State School Inspection.

Promoting quality teaching

From 2002, teachers have become public service employees with associated qualification requirements, in order to decrease the employment of unqualified and inexpert teachers in primary and secondary schools. Performance standards for general education subjects and for secondary vocational education were included in the basic pedagogical documents. New concepts for secondary school graduation and final exams have been developed. The school inspection service has started to publish reports on results in selected subjects at primary and secondary schools together with recommendations for schools.

Rethinking tertiary education in a global economy

Implementation of the Bologna strategy in the new 2002 Act on universities creates the prerequisites for increasing the mobility of students, teachers and researchers. Further support of common activities in the area of joint study programmes, in the recognition of study results and in science would help to deepen international co-operation in globalising university education and expand access to a globalising labour market.

UNITED KINGDOM

Promoting lifelong learning and improving its linkages with other socio-economic policies

The 2003 Skills Strategy set out a cross-government programme to tackle skills gaps. Progress includes 12 Employer Training Pilots delivering tailor-made training for low-skilled employees and an Adult Learning Grant to support adults studying for their first qualification equivalent to completion of upper secondary education. The New Deal for Skills will offer new ways of tackling the barriers between welfare and workforce development and draw in those with low, or no skills, on the margins of work.

Evaluating and improving outcomes of education

The government is more closely aligning teachers' skills in assessment for learning and richer data on pupil performance with intelligent systems of accountability. These systems involve effective self-evaluation, a sharper but lighter touch, external inspection, and review and support through an experienced head teacher. The Primary Education strategy for England "Excellence and Enjoyment" was launched in May 2003.

Promoting quality teaching

In England school workforce remodelling is allowing teachers more time to concentrate on their core professional responsibilities and to focus on personalised teaching and learning for all pupils.

Rethinking tertiary education in a global economy

In January 2003 the government published a strategy to give universities the investment and freedom they need to compete with the best in the world, while protecting the poorest students, and widening participation. From 2006, universities may charge up to £3 000 per year in fees. Students can pay their fees after graduation, and 30% of the poorest full time students will be guaranteed at least £3 000 in grants and bursaries per year in addition to low-interest student loans. Institutions must have strategies for increasing access before they are allowed to increase their fees. In Northern Ireland a public consultation on proposals to increase funding of higher education is underway.

Building social cohesion through education

Since April 2004, all 3- and 4-year-olds are entitled to a free part-time (two and a half hours daily) early education place if their parents want one. A Children's Workforce Unit has been created, bringing together responsibility for a number of sectors of the children's workforce.

Building new futures for education

Building Schools for the Future launches in 2005-06 with £2.2 billion of investment to start renewing all secondary schools in England to 21st century standards. An extended National Learning Network programme is supporting colleges in technical infrastructure, e-learning content and staff development.

For further information: *www.dfes.gov.uk/*

EDUCATION POLICY ANALYSIS
Purposes and previous editions

The *Education Policy Analysis* series was launched by the OECD in 1996. It forms part of the work programme of the OECD Education Committee, and responds to the policy priorities established by OECD Education Ministers. The series is prepared by the Education and Training Division of the OECD Directorate for Education.

Purposes

The main purposes of *Education Policy Analysis* are:

• To assist education policy-makers and others concerned with education policy to make better decisions by drawing on international and comparative work;

• To draw out the key insights and policy implications arising from OECD education activities, international data and indicators, and related studies; and

• To present findings, analyses and discussion in a succinct and accessible form.

Education Policy Analysis is produced annually (except in 2000, when a special edition was being prepared for the 2001 OECD Education Ministerial meeting).

Contents of the previous editions

2003

2002

2001

1999

1998

1997

1996

OECD PUBLICATIONS, 2, rue André-Pascal, 75775 PARIS CEDEX 16
PRINTED IN FRANCE
(96 2005 01 1 P) – ISBN 92-64-01865-4 - No. 53737 2005